RICHMOND PARK

Portrait of a Royal Playground

by

PAMELA FLETCHER JONES

With line illustrations
by Norman Fletcher Jones

PHILLIMORE
London and Chichester

1972

Published by

PHILLIMORE & CO. LTD.,
Shopwyke Hall, Chichester, Sussex.

SBN 85033 033 5

Text set in 11 pt. Baskerville
Printed by Unwin Brothers Ltd., Old Woking, Surrey.

To Geoffrey Wilson who suggested
this book and gave the author
generous help and encouragement

Frontis. A shy fallow deer peeps through the tree trunks

CONTENTS

ILLUSTRATIONS

Frontispiece
A shy fallow deer peeps through the tree trunks

ACKNOWLEDGMENTS

I HAVE RECEIVED a great deal of help from several organisations and many people, to all of whom I am extremely grateful: my colleagues at the Department of the Environment, particularly those in the Royal Parks Directorate; the Deputy Keepers of the Round Room at the Public Record Office; Miss Marguerite Gollancz, County Archivist of Surrey, and the staff of the Surrey Record Office; Miss Dorothy Stroud, Assistant Curator of Sir John Soane's Museum; the Reference Section of the Richmond Public Library and Mrs. Valerie Knight, District Librarian of the East Sheen Branch. I am also indebted to the Clarendon Press for permission to reproduce in Chapter II passages from Book I of Clarendon's *History of the Rebellion.*

In particular, my thanks are due to Mr. Leslie Paton, who has allowed me to reproduce five of the old prints in his possession and made available to me his splendid collection of books and references; Mr. George Thomson, Superintendent of Richmond Park until 1971, who gave me help, advice and encouragement; and Mr. George Grafton Green, who persuaded me to study for a University of London Diploma in British History in the first place.

Harry Bloom gave unstintingly of his time and skill to produce the photographs.

FOREWORD

RICHMOND PARK, SURREY, is one of London's 10 Royal Parks, six of which (St. James's Park, Green Park, Hyde Park, Kensington Gardens, Regent's Park and Primrose Hill) are in Central London and the remaining four (Greenwich Park, Hampton Court Park, Bushy Park and Richmond Park) are on the outskirts.

Richmond Park today comprises some 2,500 acres and is 2½ miles across from north to south and from east to west. It has six carriage entrance gates round its perimeter - at Richmond, Kingston, Ham, East Sheen, Roehampton and Robin Hood (on the Kingston By-Pass) - and five footgates (Ladderstile Gate, Bog Gate, Petersham Park Gate, Cambrian Gate and Bishop's Gate). Despite its name, most of the land of Richmond Park is situated in the Parish of Mortlake, about one quarter in Richmond, some in Kingston and some in Putney.

As I shall presently show, the area of the park has changed little over the 334 years since King Charles I enclosed it in 1637, but much else *has* altered.

Today, the Park is administered by the Department of the Environment, in succession to the Ministry of Public Building and Works, the Ministry of Works, the Office of Works and the Commissioners of Works, who took over its administration officially in 1904, although they had had a good deal to do with its upkeep and maintenance for some 50 years earlier.

Few full-length books have been written on Richmond Park and they have concentrated more on its natural history and wild life then on its basic history. It is mentioned at some length in several histories of the County of Surrey, however, not always very accurately.

Richmond Park has a long and fascinating history. What follows is the effort I have made to find out the truth about it.

December, 1971.   P.F.J.

I

THE FIRST TWO RICHMOND PARKS

THE RICHMOND PARK we know today was not the first park to bear this name. The first time there is any mention of a park in the area is in a survey of the manor made on the death of Bishop Burnel in the 21st year of Edward I's reign. 'It appears' the historians, Manning and Bray, tell us, 'to have been situated on the north-west of the present Vill of Richmond, between what are now the Royal Gardens and the River.' Mention is made of a park called 'The New Park' and Victorian historians thought it was probable therefore that the original park belonging to the manor at the time of the survey had had some additions made to it, either by Henry V, when he built the Palace at Richmond, or by Henry VII, when he rebuilt it. In the time of Henry VIII, they state, 'the old and new parks were distinguished by the names of the "great" and "little" parks, the former being that which was sometimes occupied by Wolsey — after he presented his Palace at Hampton Court to the King.'

Manning and Bray had a very definite theory about these two early parks which is not shared by many historians today, including the writer. 'Which of the two parks, the old or the new, was the greater does not appear, nor are we told how long they continued separate.' they added. 'They were certainly separate in 14 James I as appears by his Grant of that date to his son Prince Charles, in which the new Park is distinctly mentioned, but were probably laid together not long afterwards, one only being noticed in the Survey of 1649, which adjoined to the Green and is said to contain 349 acres. This is that which, together with the manor, was settled on the Queen in 1626/7; and the whole of it was, at the time of the Survey (1649), called the old and little Park, because a so much larger one had then been lately made by King Charles I.'

1

But Hugh Findley, writing in the Surrey Archaeological Collections on 'The Riverside Parks at Richmond,' regards the foregoing as a complete mistake. In fact, he goes so far as to say that all Surrey historians 'from Manning and Bray to Lysons' have made the same curious mistake in regard to the riverside parks at Richmond. In Tudor times, he says, there were two parks — the Great Park in which the lodge was sited and the Little Park containing the Monastery or Priory of Henry V. He points out that Manning and Bray and Lysons, as well as later writers, have assumed that the two parks were laid together in early Stuart times because one park only is mentioned in the Parliamentary Survey of 1649. Findley asserts that this assumption is inaccurate since it was not until about 1770 that they were laid together by George III. Nor, he thinks, is it strictly accurate to say that only one park is mentioned in the 1649 survey, since both parcels of land are included separately in it. The reason for the mistake, he believes, is that there was a change of designation, Charles I having formed the New or Great Park (the Richmond Park of today) on higher ground.

Even more confusing is that fact that the Great Park of Tudor times is described in the 1649 survey as the Little Park under the heading of the Manor of Richmond. The Little Park of Tudor times is described in a separate document headed 'Sheen alias West Sheen Priory.'

Certainly, says Findley, the two parks were still separate after the Restoration and were separately surveyed, valued and sold to different purchasers under leases granted to different persons down to the Georgian period. 'The Rocque's map of 1741-45 shows that at that time the two parks were well separated by the road leading from Richmond Green to Brentford Ferry, which must have been a thoroughfare of importance in Tudor and Stuart times. However, when the ferry was supplanted in 1759 by a bridge across the river at Kew, the road became of little occasion and an act of Parliament of 1766 enabled George III to close it and lay the two parks together for the first time in history.'

Findley believes that the present Old Deer Park at Richmond and the riverside portion of Kew Gardens (amounting to about 500 acres) comprise the area of the two former parks and thus

suggests that this is where the parks lay. I can find no documentary
evidence to substantiate this, although it seems more than possible,
because of the relative positions of Old Deer Park and the
riverside portion of Kew Gardens, that it was so.

II

THE ENCLOSURE

KING CHARLES I's determined enclosure of what he called Richmond New Park in 1637 against much opposition, not only from the landowners whose lands he wanted, but from Lord Cottington, the Chancellor of the Exchequer, was one of the last straws in a list of undiplomatic royal actions which cost him his throne and ultimately his head.

In his 24 year reign, this King often seems to have done the wrong thing for the right reasons and, very occasionally, the right thing for the wrong reasons. So it was with Richmond Park. If it was not for his obstinacy and pigheadedness over the enclosure of what was to be primarily a hunting park for his private use near Henry VII's Tudor Palace of Richmond, we should not today have the priceless heritage of an incomparable park which is not only a continuing joy and relaxation to members of the public who may freely visit it, but is one of Southern England's finest nature reserves, with two large deer herds and a vast collection of English trees, some of which were standing on the land even before the park was enclosed.

Much of the area that King Charles wanted to make into a park consisted of waste ground, commons and a small portion of it Crown Lands. It had been a royal hunting ground for long before the enclosure and part of it was known as Shene Chase in the reign of Henry VIII. But nearly half the land King Charles coveted belonged to local landowners and was mostly part of the estates on which they lived. Many of these people had lived there for generations – the land was both their heritage and their livelihood – and they were naturally bitterly opposed to the King purchasing it, even for a fair price.

So politically important – and disastrous – was the King's enclosure of the park in the years just proceding the Civil War

4

that Edward Hyde, Earl of Clarendon, devoted a good deal of space to it in his 'History of the Rebellion.' His account of the whole affair begins this way. 'The King, who was excessively affected to hunting and the sports of the field, had a great desire to make a great park for red as well as fallow deer between Richmond and Hampton Court, where he had large wastes of his own and great parcels of wood, which made it very fit for the use he designed it to; but as some parishes had common in those wastes, so many gentlemen and farmers had good houses and good farms intermingled with those wastes, of their own inheritance or for lives or years; and without taking in of them into the park, it would not be of the largeness or for the use proposed. His majesty desired to purchase those lands and was very willing to buy them upon higher terms than the people could sell them at to anybody else if they had occasion to part with them, and so he employed his own surveyor and other of his officers to treat with the owners, many whereof were his own tenants whose terms would at last expire.'

Despite their opposition, a number of the tenants and landowners were prevailed on to sell in a reasonably short time—urged probably as much by the really good terms offered as by a desire to please their Sovereign.

Clarendon goes on: 'The major part of the people were in a short time prevailed with, but many very obstinately refused; and a gentleman who had the best estate, with a convenient house and gardens, would by no means part with it; and the King being as earnest to compass it, made a great noise, as if the King would take away men's estates at his own pleasure.'

From the start of the enterprise, Lord Cottington and the Bishop of London (later Archbishop Laud), who was Treasurer, were very much against it, not only because of its despotic implications at a time when the King's popularity was on the wane, but because of the expense of purchasing the land and making a brick wall round so large a piece of ground.

Clarendon bears this out: 'The bishop of London, who was Treasurer, and the lord Cottington, Chancellor of the Exchequer, were, from the first entering upon it, very averse from the design, not only for the murmur of the people but because the purchase of the land, and the making a brick-wall about so large a parcel of ground, (for it is not less than ten or twelve miles about), would cost a greater sum of money than they could easily provide, or than they thought ought to be sacrificed to such an occasion; and the lord Cottington (who was more solicited by the country people, and heard most of their murmurs) took the business most to heart, and endeavoured by all the ways he could and by frequent importunities to divert his majesty from pursuing it, and put all delays he could well do in the bargains which were to be made, till the King grew very angry with him, and told him he was resolved to go through with it, and had already caused brick to be burned, and much of the wall to be built upon his own land; upon which Cottington thought fit to acquiesce.'

When the dissenters continued to refuse to sell their land, the King had the beginning of the wall built round the proposed circuit, as a strong hint that he intended to have his way. After this clear demonstration of the King's firm intention, those holding out against selling their lands reluctantly gave in because they realised that the wall would eventually cut them off from the areas of their lands inside the park.

Clarendon reports, obviously from virtually first-hand knowledge, what happened as the situation became fraught with tension and ill-feeling: 'The building the wall before people consented to part with their land or their common looked to them as if by degrees they should be shut out from both, and increased the murmur and noise of the people who were not concerned as well as of them who were, and it was too near London not to be the common discourse; and the archbishop (who desired exceedingly that the King should be possessed as much of the hearts of the people as was possible, at least that they should have no just cause to complain) meeting with it, resolved to speak with the King of it; which he did, and received such an answer from him that he thought his majesty rather not informed enough of the inconveniences and mischiefs of the thing than positively resolved not to desist from it. Whereupon one day he took the lord Cottington aside, (being informed that he disliked it,) and, according to his natural custom, spake with great warmth against it, and told him, "he should do very well to give the King good counsel, and to withdraw him from a resolution in which his honour and his justice was so much called in question." Cottington answered him very gravely, "that the thing designed was very lawful, and he thought the King resolved very well, and, since the place lay so conveniently for his winter exercise, and that he should by it not be compelled to make so long journeys as he used to do in that season of the year for his sport, that nobody ought to dissuade him from it."

The archbishop, instead of finding a concurrence from him as he expected, seeing himself reproached upon the matter for his opinion, grew into much passion, telling him "such men as he would ruin the King, and make him lose the affections of his subjects; that for his own part, as he had begun so he would go on to dissuade the King from proceeding in so ill a counsel, and that he hoped it would appear who had been his counsellor." Cottington, glad to see him so soon hot, and resolved to inflame him more, very calmly replied to him that "he thought a man could not with a good conscience hinder the King from pursuing his resolution, and that it could not but proceed from want of affection to his person, and he was not sure that it might not be high treason." The other, upon the wildness of his discourse, in great anger asked him "Why? from whence he had received that doctrine?" He said, with the same temper, "They who did not wish the King's health could not love him; and they who went about to hinder his taking recreation which preserved his health might be thought, for aught he knew, guilty of the highest crimes." Upon which the archbishop in great rage, and with many reproaches, left him, and either presently or upon the next opportunity told the King that he now knew who was his great counsellor for making his park, and that he did not wonder that men durst not represent any arguments to the contrary, or let his majesty know how much he suffered in it, when such principles in divinity and law were laid down to terrify them; and so recounted to him the conference he had with the lord Cottington, bitterly inveighing against him and his doctrine, mentioning him with all the sharp reproaches imaginable, and beseeching his majesty that his counsel might not prevail with him, taking some pains to make his conclusions appear very false and ridiculous.

The King said no more but, "My lord, you are deceived; Cottington is too hard for you: upon my word, he hath not only dissuaded me more, and given more reasons against this business, than all the men in England have done, but hath really obstructed the work by not doing his duty as I commanded him, for which I have been very much displeased with him; you see how unjustly your passion hath transported you." By which reprehension he found how much he had been abused, and resented it accordingly.'

If Cottington's devious reason for provoking the Archbishop was to make him stop the King's plans for the park, it failed — as completely as Cottington had failed earlier.

The final pockets of local resistance were now also overcome and, in Brayley and Walford's History of Surrey, an indenture is quoted, dated 22 December 1635, between the King and several freeholders, copyholders and inhabitants of Richmond, Petersham, Ham, Kingston, Wimbledon and Mortlake. It relinquished, for the sum of £4,000, all right and title to 265 acres belonging to the manor of Petersham and 483 acres belonging to that of Ham.

More than 10s. an acre would have been a very high amount in those days when, for instance, a labourer's wages were 1s.2d. and a bricklayer's 1s.8d. a day, but many of the landowners who had sold were still extremely dissatisfied, particularly since the formation of Richmond Park reduced the tithes on their lands to nearly half their former value.

To make matters worse, Charles does not seem to have paid for all the lands he took from Mortlake. It is recorded in 1635, in Domestic State Papers now in the Public Record Office, that some of the people of Mortlake had refused to sell any of their lands to him for the park and, when Charles insisted, they showed their feelings by cutting down the bushes and young trees on the land he selected. The only recompense they seem to have received, according to Domestic State Papers, was an abatement of Ship Money a year or so later and this was as a result of a petition from the inhabitants of Mortlake, sent to the King by the Council of the Sheriff of Surrey, for a re-assessment of the Ship Money levied on their lands, since he'had taken into his Park at Richmond one half of their lands.'

What was probably the first transaction concerning the park is also in Domestic State Papers. In 1630, a warrant is recorded 'to prepare a bill for his Majesty's signature, for payment of an imprest to Edward Manning, for railing in coppices, making ponds, and cutting lawns in the new park at Richmond, and bringing a river through the same'. This river may well have been a diversion of Beverley Brook which runs through the eastern part of the park. In 1635, Edward Manning was paid £2,500 for making a brick wall and £200 for enclosing with pales a parcel of ground near Beverley Bridge, but it was not until July 1636, that a warrant – 12 lines on a tiny piece of parchment – was issued to pay him £1,500 for the work which he apparently started in 1630!

Strangely, on 13 November 1635, a payment recorded in State Papers was made to him and one Thomas Young 'in part of £20,000 for land to be taken into the new park'. How Edward Manning became involved in this transaction of land, which would seem to have belonged to Thomas Young, is a mystery, since Manning was obviously a contractor of some sort who was merely employed to do constructional and other work in the proposed park. Indeed, a Royal order was issued on 28 March 1636, to assist him to recruit labour for the work. 'To all Mayors and others the King's officers and loving subjects His Majesty intends to make a new park near Richmond, in which work there will be occasion to use many bricklayers and labourers, as also carts and carriages. The persons addressed are to assist Edward Manning in taking up the required bricklayers, labourers, carts and carriages, to paying them such allowance as is usual in like case for his Majesty's service.'

In those days, the large red, the roe deer and the small, spotted fallow deer could be found in the area of the park – the roe deer is smaller than the red deer, darker in colour and has a distinctive white rump. In 1636, a warrant was issued that the King had been informed by the Marquis Hamilton that 'the roe deer escaping out of the Old Park at Wimbledon had been killed in the woods attaching and that red deer came from Windsor Forest and Far Oak into these parts, also pheasant, partridge and other fowl fly from the New Park into the woods adjoining'. The person to whom this warrant was to be addressed was to charge his servants 'that they suffer not any person to go into his woods with any gun or engine to take or destroy the game'. If any did so, the King 'would take it as a contempt done to him and see it so punished'.

The exact day and month when the park was completed for the King's use does not seem to have been recorded, but, on 23 February 1637, a payment of £100 was authorised in Domestic State Papers to Lodowick Carlile and Humfry Rogers, the first two park keepers, for 'pease, tares and hay, for the red and fallow deer in the Great Park at Richmond'.

Certainly, by June 1637, when he formally appointed the first Ranger, Richmond New Park was ready for King Charles' use.

III

THE PARK AND THE STUARTS

THE SIGNET OFFICE Docquets of June 1637, include
King Charles I's appointment of the Earl of Portland as the first
Ranger of Richmond Park, which reads:

E. PORTLAND   A warrant to Jerome Earle of Portland
for his life of the office of Keeper of
His Majestys New Park near Richmont
(sic) in the Countie of Surrey and the
Survey and Preservation of all the Deere
and Game in the same and all necessarie
wood and underwood for browse for the
deere there as oft as it shalbe needefull
to be cutt, to be spent in the lodges of
the said Parke and not elsewhere, with a
fee of 12 pence per diem (day) payable
by His Majestys Receiver Generall of the
said County of Surrey at Michaelmas and
at Lady Day and pasture for four horses
within the said Parke, with such other
fees and rights as are taken in the like
Offices. His Majestys pleasure signified
by the Lord Cottington subscribed by
Mr. Attorney . . .

The boundaries of the New Park (it was known as the 'New
Park' until nearly the end of the 19th century) were then almost
the same as they are today. There were some 1,500 deer in it,
much woodland and open green sward and very few visible
flowers.

The Earl of Portland does not seem ever to have resided in
the park himself, but, on 6 July 1637, he was granted a warrant
by the King to spend £290 'or as much therefore as shall be

11

expedient' to build a lodge for Humfry Rogers, one of the keepers of 'the Great Park', estimated at £295 or thereabouts. In November of the same year, he was granted a further warrant to pay Humfry Rogers the sum of £290, the actual sum the latter spent on building his lodge.

There were two keepers – Humfry (or Humfrey) Rogers and Lodowick Carlile – though it is not absolutely clear whether each had a separate lodge in the park at this time. It is likely, however, that Carlile lived in the former house of Gregory Cole at the extreme north-west Petersham corner of the park and Rogers at Hartleton Farm, also in the park, on the western slopes of Spankers Hill. Both keepers were granted an annual fee of £50 in the Signet Office Docquets to commence from Lady Day, 1636, 'during the King's pleasure'.

When William Murray (who was created Earl of Dysart in 1643) petitioned the King in 1639 'in consideration of the losses sustained by the inclosure of the New Park' that the lease of the manor of Petersham, which had been made out for 27 years, might be exchanged for a grant in perpetuity of the manor, the King, rather surprisingly, granted this request. In 1651, during Cromwell's Commonwealth, Sir Lionel Tollemache and his wife, Elizabeth (who was one of the four daughters of William and Katherine Murray, and was a countess in her own right), begged allowance of their titles to Ham and Petersham manors, but there is no record of whether this was ever granted.

Charles I and his court hunted and sported in his Richmond New Park until the beginning of the Civil War in 1642. By now, the resentment and anger of the gentry whose lands he had compulsorily purchased had spread to many local people and the murmurs of discontent with so despotic a King were growing louder not only just outside the park's high walls, but farther afield, but the King continued his hunting and his sporting with his usual obstinacy.

An anonymous account of 'The Making of the Richmond New Park by Charles I', written in 1751, states that 'Care was taken in the first instance fully to shew that there was no Design of hindering or preventing the Communication between the neighbouring Towns, by properly placing Gates,' which 'greatly prevented the grievances that were feared would ensue from this Inclosure'. Gates were, in fact, placed by Charles I's orders at Richmond Hill, East Sheen, Roehampton, Wimbledon (now Robin Hood Gate), Coombe (now Ladderstile footgate) and Ham Common and stepladders were placed against the wall of the park 'for the more convenient passing and repassing of Persons of all Degrees on Foot.' The 1751 account, however, was written when the rights of way through the park were in dispute, so it cannot altogether be trusted. Other accounts, nevertheless, do make it clear that at least two rights of way across the park were kept open and that poor people were allowed to enter and gather firewood, as indeed they still are.

King Charles I was beheaded at Whitehall on January 30 1649, and the House of Commons lost no time in asserting its entire supremacy by passing acts abolishing the Kingly office, the House of Lords and the Deans and Chapters. In 1658/59, Scobell's 'Statutes of the Long Parliament' state that they declared England a Commonwealth to be governed by the representatives of the people in Parliament, they passed an act for the sale of all the personal estate of the late King, his Queen and his eldest son and then an act for the sale of all Crown lands. But from the last act, among other properties, they exempted 'the New Park near Richmond, in the County of Surrey'.

7 June 1649, was appointed a day of public thanksgiving and the Lord Mayor of London and the Common Council sent a deputation to ask the House of Commons to honour the City at dinner at Grocers' Hall on that day and that 'the City might be permitted to solemnize the Thanksgiving with the House of Commons at such church as the House of Commons should please to appoint'. The Commons accepted this invitation and appointed Christ Church, Newgate Street, for the purpose.

The occasion is described in a volume of extracts from the records of Parliament and of the Corporation of London relating to the transfer to and the possession of Richmond Park by the City of London from 1649-1660: '... On which day Cromwell, with his principal officers, the Council of State, the Speaker, and the House of Commons repaired to Christ Church, heard two sermons, and walked from the church in great state to Grocers'

Hall, where they were sumptuously entertained by the City —
upon which occasion £400 was given to the poor, and the
surplus left of the provisions.'

The outcome of this — and of all the help the City of
London had given Cromwell during the Civil War — was the
following entry set out in 1649 in the Journal of the House of
Commons. 'Resolved, &c. — that the City of London have the
New Park, in the County of Surrey, settled upon them, and
their Successors, as an Act of Favour from this House, for the
Use of the City, and their Successors: And that an Act be
brought in to this Purpose. Mr. Goodwyn, Mr. Reynolds, Mr.
Salwey, Colonel Ven, Alderman Atkins, Mr. Allen, Alderman
Wilson, and Mr. Leaman do bring in the said Act.'

With what might be described as almost indecent haste —
on 17 July — the necessary legislation was passed and the
Journal records: 'Mr. Salwey reports an Act for settling the New
Park of Richmond alias Richmond Great Park, on the Mayor and
Commonalty and Citizens of London, and their Successors for
ever. Which was read the First and Second time. A Proviso for
excepting Timber Trees out of the Bill: which was read the First
time. Resolved, &c., — That this Proviso be read the Second time.
The Proviso being read the Second time, was, upon the Question
assented unto: and ordered to be Part of the Bill. And the Act,
with that Proviso, being put to the Question, passed.'

So the executed King's expensively-won playground now
played a different role. It not only expressed the new regime's
thanks to the influential City of London, but it was an instrument
for keeping the City — and especially its wealthy merchants —
'sweet' for future use!

In the recommendations made by Parliament to the City
regarding the park, it was pointed out that it was the intention of
Parliament that Richmond New Park should be preserved as a
park still, 'without Destruction, and to remain as an ornament to
the City and a Mark of Favour from the Parliament unto the said
City'.

The Earl of Portland was no longer Ranger — he had been
arrested as a Royalist as soon as the Civil War ended and heavily
fined. He lived   quietly   at   Walton-on-Thames   during   the

Interregnum. The two keepers of the New Park were allowed to remain and the Chamberlain's Vellum Book for 1650 recorded that £100 was paid 'to Lodowick Carlile and Humfry Rogers Esquires Keeps of the New Parke neere Richmond in the County of Surry [sic] to them allowed for theire pains in keeping and looking to the said Parke.' and that they also paid Humfry Rogers £14 6s.8d. for charges disbursed by him 'in paleing and ditching some pte of New Parke as by one bill appeareth.'

During the Commonwealth, the park was looked after reasonably well and, with typical Cromwellian thoroughness, a 1649 Parliamentary survey of Richmond, Wimbledon and Nonsuch in the County of Surrey gives the following information: 'There is in the said parke one open barne or deere house of good tymber well tiled containing 4 bayes which we valew to be worth above all chardges in taking downe the same the sum of £13.6.8. There are no deere at all within the said parke for the same weare some years since destroyed.'

This last statement is particularly astonishing since, when the park was enclosed, there were about 1,500 deer in it. Although Coryn de Vere in his Handbook of Richmond Park does say that, when Charles II was restored, the park was 'nearly denuded of deer' − a questionable statement, anyway − it is more likely that this would have happened during the Interregnum, rather than during the Royalist years before it when the King would have made sure the park was well-stocked with deer for sporting purposes. It is possible, of course, that the survey was not a very thorough one and that it was done at a time of the year when the deer are particularly timid and retiring, so that counting − or even seeing − them would have been difficult.

The survey goes on: 'The timber trees and other trees now standing and growing within the said parke being in number one thousand nine hundred and fortie and six (over and besides such as are marked out for the use of the Navie) being for the most parts ould Dotrells and decayed pollard trees good for litle save the fier are worth upon the place one tree with anouther the sum of three shillings six pence farthing per tree (the time of converting them into money allsoe considered). In toto £342.11.6.

The trees within the parke aforesaid already marked out for the use of the Navie are found to bee in number ... [but no number is given]. The grose valewes of the materialls are in toto £11701.8.0. ob.' This last was, of course, an immense sum in those days — so immense that one wonders if it was accurately recorded in the survey. This doubt is upheld since the total acreage surveyed was given as only 367 and 30 perches and it was also noted that 'there are allsoe growing in divers places of the said parké divers bushes of thorne and other under wood which we valew to bee worth upon the place the sum of £030.0.0.'

The survey also places the annual value of £583 18s.0d. on 'the manor or court house of Richmond and the said parke and lodge and other before mentioned royalties and premises' which, it states, 'are in cleare possession and are tithe free as having never beene chardged therewith'.

Until the end of the Commonwealth, Rogers and Carlile were paid their £50-a-year salaries, but they also received sundry other payments, such as on 7 November 1654, when it was 'ordered by this Court that Mr. Chamblen shall pay unto the the Keepers of New Park the fees by them demanded for venison killed in the said Parke for entertainment of the Lord Protector and the Comon Councill amounting to £7.6.8.'

This is further proof that either the survey was wrong in stating that there were no deer left in the park, or it had been very thoroughly restocked in the succeeding five years. The keepers, incidentally, provided venison for the Protector and his Council on several occasions, which seems to suggest that puritanical and austere though their lives may have been, they still enjoyed 'a royal meal' occasionally!

Among other payments to the keepers in 1654, noted in the Chamberlain's Vellum Book was £58 13s. 3d. 'for assessments towards the maintenance of the Army £56.0.14 [sic] and for the providing of a County Goale 52s.1d.'. It would seem - as in the two World Wars of the 20th century - that the Army was stationed in the park during this period, for, in 1655, the keepers were paid £35 2s. 2d. for nine months' maintenance and, on 15 July 1656, an order was made 'that the Keepers of new Park be disbursed their charge for quartering soldiers for non-payment of the assessment taxed upon the said park'.

In 1656, too, they received, with other payments, 6s. towards 'the repaire of the County Goale' – what the keepers of the park had to do with the County Goal remains a mystery– and two more payments 'for quartering of Souldiers' totalling £18 19s. 9d. In 1657, the Park seems to have given hospitality to the Navy as well as the Army, since, among a number of payments to the keepers, we find a sum of £71 3s. 2d. for 15 months' assessments towards 'the maintenance of the Army and Navy ended the 24th of June 1657' and, in 1658, they received £39 17s. 6d. towards the maintenance of the Army and Navy until Lady Day of that year. After that, as the Commonwealth began to break up, it is probable that the Army and Navy were no longer billeted in the park, because there are no more records of payments for their upkeep to the two keepers.

Throughout the Interregnum, Rogers and Carlile were paid, though not always fully, for any repairs they did to their own lodges - which suggests that they now had one each - and to the park itself, particularly to the outer wall, which, as breaches appeared in it, needed constant rebuilding, mainly so that the deer might not escape.

On the other hand, the keepers now had to pay £220 rent to the City annually for 'Pannage agistments grass hay gorse or furrs bushes or yearly proffitts groweing being or made off in out off or upon the said Parke or grounds or any part thereof (excepting the goeing depasturing Feeding and keeping of 1300 Fallow deere and 200 Red deere in and upon the said Parke yearely &c)'.

So it seems clear that, by 1652 when the first payment was made, the park had either been restocked with 1,500 deer or many of that number had never been lost despite what had been stated in the 1649 survey. That there must have been a certain amount of restocking *is* clear from the payments recorded in the Chamberlain's Vellum Book for 1650 as being made to Carewe Rawleigh esquire for 'CXXXIII^{tie}' head of 'Fallowe Deare at XXs p head of him bought and by him delivered out of his Parke called Kempton Parke into the Citties Parke called New Parke neere Kingstone in the County of Surrey' and to Captain William Disher for 'the deere for New Parke' delivered 'according to agreement' in May 1651 and in March 1654/5. But since Captain Disher was paid only £100 for the 1651 delivery and about the same for the later one and Carewe Rawleigh was charging £1 a head for the 133 deer *he* supplied, it would seem likely that Captain Disher did not supply more than 200 head of deer altogether which, even with breeding, would not account for the total of 1,500! In any case, Captain Disher's second delivery of deer was not made until *after* 1652 when this number was quoted.

By 1659, time was running out, not only for the Commonwealth, but for the City of London's ownership of Richmond New Park. As the first positive rumblings of the returning Monarchy were heard in London's still prosperous City, it would seem that it was born in on the City fathers that, for their continuing prosperity, it might be as well to change their coats rather hastily. This decision must have been strengthened after a long letter, dated 14 April 1660, was received by the Lord Mayor and Aldermen of London from King Charles II, who was still at Breda in Holland. Considering the hand the City had had in expelling Charles II's father, the City Corporation must have been very relieved indeed to receive this most cordial letter. Certainly it lost no time in sending 14 of its most important members to attend His Majesty at the Hague, where he received them and knighted them all. Substantial proof of the City's fervent, not to say extravagant, loyalty was the £12,000 carried by the deputation to the King and the restoration to him and his heirs of Richmond New Park.

King Charles II landed in England on 29 May 1660, to claim his inheritance, but 22 days earlier, with the almost indecent haste with which Cromwell had given it to *them*, the City restored Richmond Park to him. An order made in the Common Council and recorded in its Journal on May 7 proclaimed: 'Ordered by this Court that the Right Honourable the Lord Mayor doe at the first opportunity of his Matyes comeinge to this City in the name thereof and of this court, present the newe Parke to his Majesty and informe his Majesty that this Citty hath beene only his Matyes stewards for the same. And it is ordered that in the meanetyme the deere and woods therein bee preserved.'

On 2 June 1660, it was reported in the Common Council by Mr. Recorder that 'himselfe and the right Honourable the Lord Maior together with the Aldermen had this afternoone attended his Majesty in order to congratulate his Majestye's Restauracon and likewise to present the Newe Parke to his Majesty according to a late vote of this Court and that he did declare it was done by way of restitution and not gift and further said it was well it was in the Citty's hands for that they had preserved the wood vert and game. Whereupon his Matye returned answeare that the Citty of London were still loading him with their kindness and that he looked uppon the said Parke to be kept for him and that hee accepted it not as restored but as freely given unto him by the Citty and thanked them for the same'.

And with this typically urbane reply, the kindly, but cynical King, whom 15 years' exile and privation must have made a very good judge of character — though it seems never to have made him bitter — accepted, very much at its face value, the City of London's hurried return to him of the Park that his unfortunate father had completed 23 years earlier.

This second Royal Charles was very different from the first, although they were father and son. Of a much more easy-going and philosphical nature, Charles II returned to the land of his birth with one strong determination — *not,* through obstinacy and shortsightedness, to follow his father to the scaffold. Throughout his 25 years on the throne, he managed, sometimes precariously and often financially insolvent, to keep an even balance between himself, his peers, the political parties and the ordinary folk of England, who soon came to regard him as the first monarch who cared about them as human beings. And if his great charm and warmth, which may have masked a certain indolence of purpose, sometimes made people believe that he cared about them and their affairs more than he really did, they mostly accepted his promises, even if they were never implemented, with good humour.

The King must certainly have made a number of promises to the loyalists who stood by him in those wandering years and, no doubt, he meant those promises in good faith. But circumstances sometimes stopped him honouring them. So it may well have been with Sir Daniel Harvey (or Hervey), Bart. Though no record can be found of it, Sir Daniel must have been certain the King intended him to be the first post-Restoration Ranger and Keeper of Richmond New Park and, without waiting for anything official (or, if he had it, there is no record of it), tried to take over his office forthwith. But Elizabeth, Countess of Dysart, now married to Sir Lionel Tollemache, had been biding her time. It must have seemed reasonable to her that, since Charles I had taken much of her father's land to make the park, that her father had also been a knight of the bedchamber to him and that he and his family had remained loyal to the Monarchy, if quietly, during the Commonwealth, the Rangership should now belong to her and her husband. She must have made this very clear to the unfortunate Sir Daniel Harvey, because, in the early summer of 1660, Sir Daniel sent a petition to the King 'to refer to his counsel-at-law the contract to his title to the Rangership of the New Park, wherein he is obstructed by the eldest daughter of William Murray, Earl of Dysart one of the bedchamber of the Late King, married to Sir Lionel Tollemache who pretends an interest in the same. With reference thereto to the attorney and solicitor general'.

But Lady Dysart's claim must have also seemed reasonable to the King, because, in July 1660, he made a 'Grant with survivorship to Sir Lionel Tollemache, Bart and Elizabeth, his wife, Countess of Dysart, of the office of keeping the New Park, Richmond, Co. Surrey, and overseeing and preserving the deer there; fee 1s. a day'. which was recorded both in Domestic State Papers and in the Signet Office Docquet Book.

Apparently to propitiate Sir Daniel, who must still have been angrily demanding justice, the King, in August 1660, granted 'To Sir Daniel Harvey *after* Sir Lionel Tollemache and his lady of the custody of the New Park near Richmond, Surrey'. Since Sir Lionel and his lady were still fairly young, this promise must have been little comfort to Sir Daniel and he must have continued to petition the King, because, on 19 July 1661, he, with Ralph Montague, was granted with survivorship the office of keeper of Hartleton Lodge and Walk in Richmond Park.

1. Unusual view of one of the Pen Ponds

2 and 3. Two views of Pembroke Lodge. Above, the front. On the right of the picture what remains of the original Molecatcher's Cottage can be seen. Below, the back. The Lodge is now a public restaurant and part of its back garden is used as an open air eating area. From here, there is a magnificent view of the Petersham Park area of the park.

4. Light and shade on a summer day

5. Aquatic scene in the Isabella Woodland Garden

6. Rural scene near Ham Gate

7. Ham Pond

To have been made a kind of superior lodgekeeper, when he expected to be Ranger, cannot have pleased Sir Daniel overmuch. One suspects that he went on crying to the King for justice. As well as writing to him officially, there is little doubt that he must have approached him personally several times, for Charles was surprisingly accessible to his subjects, especially to those more highly placed.

Humfry Rogers, who, as keeper of the park at the end of the Commonwealth, still lived in Hartleton Lodge (or Farm), had surrendered it on 23 July 1661, under letters patent. Lodowick Carliell [sic] did not, with his son, James, have to surrender Petersham House (or Lodge) until 13 April 1663, when his keepership was granted to Thomas Panton and Bernard Greenville.

On 23 July 1664, a fee of £50 per annum was directed to be paid to Sir Daniell Harvy [sic] and Ralph Montague, presumably jointly, for their custody of Hartleton Lodge and Walk and the same fee to Thomas Panton and Bernard Greenville.

There seems to be no record of Harvey, Montague, Panton and Greenville being paid before 1664, although it is likely that their payments were back-dated. Nevertheless, three years seem a very long time for Sir Daniel and Ralph Montague to have waited for their first payment, especially since they appear to be receiving jointly only the same sum that the previous keeper of each lodge had been paid.

It can only be surmised whether what happened next was the result of the King's desire to put a long distance between himself and someone who constantly nagged him — probably both at court and as he took his daily walk, with his attractive following of little spaniel dogs, along what came to be known, because of the purpose to which he put it, as Constitution Hill. Charles was extremely human and was not one for putting up with being made uncomfortable for very long! One would like to think that he genuinely believed that Sir Daniel was particularly well-equipped for the job he gave him. Whatever the reason, on 28 December 1667, the King appointed Sir Daniel Harvey Ambassador to the Ottoman Empire! One can imagine Sir Daniel's consternation on learning about his new job — quickly masked if the King broke the news to him personally, though the easy-going

Monarch was far more likely to have avoided the persistent Sir Daniel and have written to him instead!

Whichever way he received the news, Sir Daniel must have shown great reluctance to take up his appointment because, on 10 June 1668, a letter is recorded in Domestic State Papers from the King to his brother, the Duke of York and Lord High Admiral, that he had directed Sir Daniel Harvey to sail for Smyrna, Turkey, forthwith.

The reason for Sir Daniel's delay *could* have been that Sir Lionel Tollemache had died early in 1668 and, at last, Sir Daniel had become the Ranger of Richmond New Park, despite the Countess of Dysart having been granted survivorship after her husband. That he actually took up office seems to be proved by an entry in the Domestic State Papers in 1668 when Sir Daniel reported to the King about the repairs necessary in 'the Park under my charge (New Park?) which is the Best Park that is left, for reserving and preserving the deer, etc., no groom or houndsman should be allowed a key, as they sell the fawns, nor should the serjeants of the buckhouses have access when His Majesty is not there, as they kill the deer, instead of training the hounds'.

Records disagree on the year of Sir Lionel's death - some give it as 1669 in France. If this is so, it would suggest that Sir Daniel did *not* become Ranger in 1668 and this seems unlikely in view of the foregoing entry in State Papers. It is possible that Elizabeth, Countess of Dysart, may have continued as Ranger after her first husband's death, but this, too, seems unlikely because there is no record of any payments to her or transactions she made concerning the park during the period before her second husband became Ranger in 1673.

Eventually – albeit reluctantly – Sir Daniel set sail in *The Leopard* from Deal, Kent, for Turkey on 15 August 1668, putting into Plymouth on the way on 25 August where he was delayed by cross winds. He must eventually have arrived in Turkey in the autumn of that year, because a letter sent to him by the Levant Company, dated 31 May 1669, thanks him for letters of December 1668, and February 1669, and congratulates him on his safe arrival.

He may well have been allowed to leave his wife, Lady

Harvey, as Rangèr in his stead, because on 8 January 1669, a warrant to pay her and Colonel Thomas Panton £100 for providing hay for the deer in the New Park was issued. It could be argued that this may have been because they were lodgekeepers, but this seems unlikely since previously there are no records of similar payments to them. But poor Sir Daniel never saw his wife or Richmond Park again, because he died in the Ottoman Empire in 1672 without ever having returned to England.

On 17 February 1672, four years after her first husband's death, the widowed Elizabeth, Countess of Dysart, married John Maitland, Earl (later the 1st Duke) of Lauderdale in Petersham Church and Charles II made him Ranger of Richmond Park in May 1673, with a fee, recorded in the Signet Office Docquet Book, of six shillings a day. Once again, Lady Dysart was the wife of the Ranger.

The state of the park was good during the 13 years since Charles II's Restoration. By 1660, it is recorded in State Papers there were 2,000 deer, some of them animals collected from France and various private enclosures to augment his own herds by the King, though by 1669 State Papers record only 600 animals left. While, since Charles still used the park as a private hunting reservation, a good many may have been sacrificed to the court hunters and not replaced, it is also possible that they were decimated by disease.

Late in 1660, Sir Lionel Tollemache petitioned the King to be 'made a judge of what should be allowed to the underkeepers. They claim beside their £50 fee, the keeping of 24 cows and 10 horses each and the mowing of 60 acres of grass; if this is allowed there will be a yearly expense to provide hay for the deer'.

There is no record of whether Sir Lionel's petition was granted, but it seems likely that the perquisites of succeeding keepers in the park were curtailed and certainly the rights of pasturage and keeping animals in later generations were much smaller, although they survived right up to the beginning of the 20th century.

Mention is first made of the park in John Aubrey's *Natural History and Antiquities of the County of Surrey*, the first volume of which was published in 1673. A brief reference says: 'By the road to Kingston (north) is New Park (one of the best parks in England) made in the time of King Charles the First. Some of the workmen that made the brick wall that encloseth it, did aver to me, that it is Eleven miles in Compass.'

The Duke of Lauderdale died either at the end of 1682 or the beginning of 1683 and, in October 1683, Laurence Hyde, Earl of Rochester, brother-in-law of the Duke of York and second son of the great Earl of Clarendon, was appointed Ranger. His citation was fuller than earlier ones and, rather strangely, it commenced 'A grant unto Laurence Earle of Rochester and his heirs and assisgnes for the lives of the Ld. Huntingtowne and Thomas Panton Esqe and the longer liver of them and afterwards during His Majesty's pleasure ...'. As well as, in common with earlier Rangers, being granted 'the herbage and pannage of the said parke beyond what shall be sufficient for the deer and game and the browswood and windfall wood and dead trees and chiminage within the said Parke,' the Earl of Rochester was granted 'the liberty to plant trees against the wall of the said Parke or any part thereof, with all other profits and advantages to the said office belonging' and a fee of 'three bucks and three does in every season' in addition to his six shillings a day.

Elizabeth, Duchess of Lauderdale, who had been excluded yet again from the Rangership although she had been granted the right of survivorship in 1660, lived on until 1698 and was buried at Petersham.

In 1685 King James II came to the throne and, during his disastrous three years as monarch which ended with the Bloodless Revolution in 1688, he found time to re-affirm the Rangership of his brother-in-law. He even increased his fees by 30 pence a day and, in addition, he extended the Rangership to Henry, Viscount Hyde, the Earl of Rochester's eldest son, for the period of the latter's life.

The Earl of Rochester continued as Ranger through the reign of William III and Mary and it was they who made the public's entry to the park much easier. Ordinary people could still not wander at will, but those on foot could walk through the park, even if they were not using it as a thoroughfare (as was the public's right), though they could not ride or take a vehicle through it without a special permit. The reason for this may have been greater royal tolerance or it may have been the fact that Dutch William was anything but a lighthearted hunting man and probably did not often put the park to its original use.

On at least one occasion, however, the King certainly hunted in the park for, in 1696, two men, Sir William Parkyns and Sir John Friend, were sentenced to be executed for conspiracy to kill the King on his return from hunting in Richmond Park 'in a narrow and winding lane leading from the landing place on the north of the river (at Strand-on-the-Green) where he crossed by boat on his way through Turnham Green to Kensington Palace'.

In 1702, when Queen Anne came to the throne, she appointed Laurence, Earl of Rochester, her Lieutenant General and Governor General of the Kingdom of Ireland, but he still continued as Ranger.

The following year, she granted to James, Duke of Ormand, a 99-year lease 'of all that mansion house usually called The Lodge and several clauses and parcells of lands thereto belonging and within the Park called or known by the name of Richmond Old Parke in the County of Surrey and also of several other clauses and parcells of land within the Mannor of Richmond at West Sheen in the said County of Surrey' at the yearly rents of £13 4s.0d. and £14 6s.8d. It seems unlikely that this deed referred to Richmond *New* Park and thus partly supports Hugh Findley's contention, noted in Chapter I, that the two old Richmond Parks were still existing separately into the reigns of the Georges.

In 1711, Laurence, Earl of Rochester, died and was succeeded by his son, Henry (known as Harry) Hyde, who had been granted the Rangership after his father's death by James II. In September 1711, Queen Anne confirmed this, but allowed him to sub-grant the office jointly to Francis Gwyn, Esqre and Richard Powys, gent, 'to hold the said office to whom the said Francis Gwyn and Richard Powys, their heirs and assigns'.

It is almost certain that Messrs. Powys and Gwyn paid the new Earl of Rochester well for the privilege of taking over the

Rangership, in which the Earl cannot have been very interested —
or, at any rate, he was more interested in money! Queen Anne
further stipulated that, after the Earl of Rochester's death, Gwyn
and Powys were to surrender the office to his son and heir, Henry
Hyde, Esqre (commonly called Henry, Viscount Hyde) and
William Leveson Gower.

Despite the fact that he had officially given up his interest
in the park, the 2nd Earl of Rochester is mentioned in its
connection three times in Treasury Papers between 1713 and
and 1723. In 1713, he protested when trees were to be felled in
the park to build a chapel on to the church on Kew Green,
fearing that it might deface the park, and, 10 years later,
protested again for the same reason when it was proposed to
raise £2,000 for the Exchequer by felling more trees. In
September 1716, he also sent in a request that the park walls,
land drains and buildings should be repaired at an estimated cost
of £840 without timber, but only £380 was allowed.

Brayley and Walford in Volume II of the *History of Surrey*
state that 'Queen Anne demised the office for three lives to her
uncle, Laurence Hyde, Earl of Rochester (died 1711), and his son
and heir, who had succeeded to the Earldom of Clarendon, joined
with his son, Lord Cornbury, in a sale of the grant and remainder
to George I for £5,000' but I can find no documentary evidence
for this last statement or, indeed, for the 'three lives' statement.

IV

ONWARDS FROM GEORGE I

THE SECOND EARL of Rochester (now Clarendon) lived until 1727, when two Georges had already ascended the throne and, on his death, George II appointed to the Rangership 'for and during his Majesty's pleasure' Robert, Lord Walpole, the son of his favourite Prime Minister, Sir Robert Walpole. Like his two predecessors, Lord Walpole was to have three bucks and three does every season and 6s. a day — the extra 30 pence seems only to have been given to the 1st Earl of Rochester in James II's reign.

In 1740, George II issued an amendment to this appointment. It granted Robert, Lord Walpole, the Rangership for his lifetime and, if his father should survive him, he was to take over the Rangership for the remainder of his life. In fact, Sir Robert Walpole died in 1745, six years before his son. Both Walpoles took an active interest in the park; both were keen on hunting, the father particularly so.

It was obvious and currently thought that though Lord Walpole was nominally the Ranger, his father actually held the position and it seems very probably that the King added the amendment to ensure that his Prime Minister could continue to enjoy the park throughout his life.

Sir Robert Walpole used to go regularly to the Old Lodge in the park to stay at weekends and to hunt, and Lord Hervey twice mentions in his memoirs that the Prime Minister had to be sent for from Richmond Park when the Queen (Caroline) wanted him urgently. On the first occasion, in 1736, he does not seem to have been alone there, since Lord Hervey writes: 'Sir Robert Walpole was gone to Richmond Park (which, by the way, the Queen did not take very well), so Lord Hervey [he wrote his memoirs in the third person] despatched a messenger immediately

27

to him to let him know the good news [that King George II was safe at Helvoetsluys in Holland], but did not venture to tell him that he found the Queen looked upon his retirement with Miss Skerrett to Richmond Park just at this juncture as a piece of gallantry which, considering the anxiety in which he left Her Majesty, might have been spared, as well as the gallantry of His Majesty's journey to Hanover which had occasioned that anxiety.'

The Prime Minister insisted that at the weekends in Richmond Park he did more business 'than he could in town' and the *Dictionary of National Biography* states that the closing of the House of Commons on Saturdays dates from this period!

In the Surrey edition of the *Victoria County Histories*, it is pointed out that 'The Prime Minister, although he effected improvements and spent much money on the Park, made several infringements on the rights of the public by shutting up gates and taking away stepladders on the walls'. He probably felt that since he had spent a good deal of money on the park and *was* the Prime Minister, he was entitled to more privacy. For whatever reason, he also built lodges at the gates with keepers in them whose orders — according to his son, Horace Walpole's *Memoirs of the Reign of King George II* — were 'to admit all respectable persons in the daytime and such carriages as had tickets, which were easily obtained'. State Papers record that the lodge at Ham Gate, for instance, was built in 1742.

After Sir Robert's death, his son continued the same policy.

In 1749, George II, who had already granted to his favourite and youngest daughter, Amelia (or Amelie), 'the offices of Keeper and Paler of the House Park of Hampton Court and the Manor of the Brakes there for her life' in 1747, appointed her, in Patent Rolls, Ranger of Richmond New Park in reversion on the death of Robert, Earl of Orford (Lord Walpole) during her lifetime.

Lord Orford died in 1751 and Princess Amelia, who had been living at Dutch House, Hampton Court, vacated it and took up residence in the park at White Lodge, which had been built by her father as a retreat for himself, his Queen and the royal family about 1728 and was, for some years, known as The Stone Lodge. It was a favourite resort of Queen Caroline and the broad, oak-bordered ride on its eastern side, which was one of her special haunts, was named 'The Queen's Ride' in her honour. While Princess Amelia lived at White Lodge, she caused the building of two brick wings to be started, but they were not finished when she left the park in 1761.

Very shortly after taking up her appointment, Princess Amelia closed the park to the public and refused admission except to her personal friends and those few others with special permits, which were *not* easy to obtain. One historian records that she refused an entrance key to the park even to Lord Chancellor Hardwicke and Lord Brooke.

She also attempted to stop up an old road from Kingston, through Richmond to Shene and, in 1756, there is a report in Treasury Board Papers, from the Attorney General to the King, of a way and path through Richmond Park which had been closed as a public footpath. That Princess Amelia was determined to have as little as possible to do with the public is further emphasised by another entry, later in the same year, in which she requested that the warrant for the erection of stiles and ladders against the wall of 'the New Park near Richmond Gate' might be directed to the 'proper officer' and not to her.

When Princess Amelia excluded the public from the park in 1751, local people went so far, when she herself was adamant, as to petition the Lord Chancellor, but their petitions were refused. In 1754, an action was brought against the Deputy Ranger, James Shaw, because a gatekeeper, Deborah Burgess, had refused admission to a number of gentlemen led by a Mr. Symons, but the verdict was given against the plaintiffs in a two-day trial before the Lord Chief Justice and a jury, in which it was asserted by 37 witnesses for the defence that anyone who was willing to pay 2s.6d. for a key could get into the park.

The following year, John Lewis, a brewer of Richmond and a most public spirited man, deliberately tried to enter the park when a carriage was passing through Sheen Gate. When Martha Gray, the gatekeeper there, refused him permission to enter without a ticket, he protested that the public had a right of way. When she still demanded a ticket, he tried to force his way through, but Martha Gray pushed him out and locked the gate. Single-handed, he then proceeded to bring an action against the gatekeeper, which was, in fact, an action against the Ranger, Princess Amelia. The Crown avoided the trial for three years and then there was difficulty in empanelling a jury, but eventually the case was heard at Surrey Assizes at Kingston on 3 April 1758, before Sir Michael Foster and with Sir John Phillips, of Milford, Co. Pembroke, as the leading counsel. Lewis based his case on the rights of way for pedestrians granted by Charles I and not, as in the previous action, for unrestricted entry for both pedestrians and vehicles. He won the case.

Asked by the Judge whether he would have admission by gates or step ladders, he said ladders, since gate keys could be lost! Forced to put up ladder-stiles, the Princess angrily made sure they had very widely-spaced rungs which made them extremely difficult to use, so Lewis again applied to the court and the Judge ordered that the rungs of the ladders were to be no farther apart than could be used by old people and children.

A third action, in 1760, however, to secure the rights of admission for carriages without tickets, went in favour of the Crown.

Probably because of the vast expenses he incurred on the law suits, plus the flooding of his brewery and countinghouse when the River Thames overflowed at Petersham and washed away all his business books and papers, John Lewis fell into great poverty in later life. The local parson, Thomas Wakefield, who had been very much involved in the campaign for the rights of way for the public in the park, persuaded the residents of Richmond to contribute to a small annuity for him and on this he managed to survive for a number of years.

John Lewis died on 22 October 1792, and was buried in his family vault in the churchyard of Richmond Parish Church. There is evidence that the memorial was still there until the late 1950s, but when the churchyard, which was very overgrown, was cleared, it must have been removed and no trace of it remains. His memory is perpetuated, however, by an oil painting which hangs in Richmond Public Library painted by T. Stewart, a pupil of Sir Joshua Reynolds. An engraving of this picture, published in 1793, bears the inscription: 'Be it remembered that by the Steady

Perseverance of John Lewis Brewer at Richmond Surry, the Right of a Free Passage through Richmond Park was recovered and established by the Laws of this Country (notwithstanding very strongly opposed) after being upwards of twenty years withheld from the People.'

In 1761, her father now dead and her nephew on the throne, Princess Amelia who had become very unpopular indeed in and around Richmond Park and had, because she had not managed to keep the public out of the park, lost interest in it, left White Lodge and surrendered the Rangership and, it is believed, went to live at Gunnersbury.

She may, however, have left for posterity and the enjoyment of future generations one deed to her credit. She is said to have formed Pen Ponds from 10 acres of old gravel pits in the park, though, as will be shown in the next chapter, it is by no means certain that she did much more than re-name the ponds.

Although in the Docquet Book, King George III described Princess Amelia as his 'beloved aunt' when she surrendered the Rangership, he was undoubtedly secretly delighted that such a trouble-maker should leave Richmond Park, because George III really loved the park and did a good deal for it. He now appointed John, Earl of Bute, his favourite minister and later Prime Minister, Ranger, which office Bute kept until his death in 1792. Lord Bute lived at White Lodge during his Rangership, though whether he lived in the Park permanently or visited it only at weekends, as Sir Robert Walpole had, is not clear.

The King's interest continued throughout Bute's Rangership. For instance, in 1761, it is recorded in State Papers Domestic that that repairs and works were executed 'under the King's own eye' by the Board of Works.

That the park now had other less welcome visitors than the law-abiding public is illustrated by an account of a Mrs. Mann, sister-in-law of Sir Horace Mann, a friend of Horace Walpole, in in whose letters the story is told. In November 1782, Mrs. Mann 'was robbed in New Park, between three and four in the afternoon. The prudent matron gave the highwayman a purse with very little money, but slipped her watch into the bag of the coach'.

After the Earl of Bute's death, George III took over the Rangership himself. He was the first monarch — there were, in fact, only two — to do so. Until 1814, when his mental state, now thought to be due to porphyria, caused him to give up the office, he administered the park with great interest and good sense. In 'The Environs of London,' Lysons tells us 'His Majesty... has it in contemplation to cause all the swampy parts to be effectually drained, the rough banks to be levelled, and the roads turned where beauty and advantage may be gained by so doing. The open parts, especially the large tract of ground towards East Sheen, are to be ornamented with plantations adapted to the elevation of the surface; and the vallies opened so as to carry the appearance of greater extent, and to give additional grandeur to the old plantations. Within the walls of the park is an eligible and compact farm of 225 acres. To this it is said that His Majesty, who has shown a very laudable zeal for the encouragement and improvement of agriculture, will pay particular attention'.

Alas, George III, for all his enthusiasm, did not carry out all or, indeed, a very great deal of this ambitious programme, but it is recorded in 'A general view of the Agriculture of Surrey' written in 1794 by James and Malcolm, that, very shortly after 1792, an attempt *was* made to grow cereals in the park. At first, the land yielded good crops, especially of oats, but later the thin, hungry, gravelly soil and the inroads of deer, etc., made it advisable to lay it down again as a permanent pasture.

In 1798, the King put up the present gates and built the lodge at the Richmond Hill entrance to the park. The iron gates still bear the date they were erected and the initials 'G.R.' and 'C.R.' for the King and Charlotte, his Queen. Whenever the Richmond gates and lodge have been mentioned in earlier works on the park, they have been attributed to Capability Brown, but I can find no evidence to support this contention.

It is true that Lancelot — or Capability — Brown did a great deal of landscape and associated design for King George III, much of it at Hampton Court where, from 1764 until his death, he was Surveyor to His Majesty's Gardens and Waters. But Brown died in 1783, 15 years before the gates and lodge were erected, if the date on the gates is correct. This is, of course, no proof that he did *not* design the gates and lodge years earlier, but Miss Dorothy Stroud, his biographer, could find no reference to them in her researches or in his only surviving account book which is fairly detailed.

What Miss Stroud *has* found is a plan by the great architect, Sir John Soane (of whom she is also biographer) of 'the intended lodge and gate on Richmond Hill' which are similar to those at the Richmond entrance today. Soane was appointed Deputy Surveyor of Woods and Forests in 1795. Miss Stroud believes that he probably put up the gates before then and built the lodge *after* his appointment, since it was noted on the plan that the lodge was approved by George III on 14 September 1795. This work was probably done as part of Soane's official duties; there is no specific mention of the lodge in his bill book of works at Richmond, as one would have expected had the work been done in a private capacity. The plan is preserved in Sir John Soane's Museum, of which Miss Stroud is Assistant Curator, in Lincoln's Inn Fields.

At this time, the turn of the 19th century, a great many domestic animals were kept in the park. In 1806, for instance, there were 400 sheep and 300 lambs at the Ranger's Farm (known as King's Farm) and 89 cows or oxen at large in the park, the latter being the property of the Ranger, the park staff and the residents of the lodges. Oddly enough, only seven horses are mentioned in a contemporary list.

Viscount Sidmouth (the politician Henry Addington) had been living in White Lodge since 1801 and, in 1813, the King made him Deputy Ranger. He continued as Deputy Ranger in the next Rangership and partly during the following one and died at White Lodge in 1844. During his occupation of the house, he was visited there by many eminent men including Sheridan, the younger Pitt, Sir Walter Scott and, perhaps the most distinguished of all, on 10 September 1805, Admiral Lord Nelson. This was just five weeks before the Battle of Trafalgar and Nelson's death and it is said that the Admiral sketched out with wine on a table at White Lodge the plan by which he proposed to break the enemy's lines. The table, with a bronze plaque on it recording the Nelson incident, is no longer at White Lodge, but certainly up to the end of the 19th century it was preserved at Upottery Manor in Devon.

Lord Sidmouth gave his name to Sidmouth Wood, which is today a bird sanctuary.

The Prince of Wales was already Regent when Princess Elizabeth, the next Ranger, was appointed. Although the appointment was made in the name of George III, it seems probable that she was chosen by her brother, rather than her father who was by then very ill. It is unlikely that the Princess took a very great interest in her charge, but Lord Sidmouth did and, although officially only Deputy, for practical purposes he was really the Ranger.

In addition to Sidmouth Wood, he enclosed Spankers Hill Wood and the Isabella Plantation and a number of smaller enclosures. He also trained the park staff with great intelligence. In 1824, for instance, when at Richmond Gate, the large iron gates had to be opened to receive carriages entering the park, a contemporary account records that: 'Upon ringing a bell and producing an order from the Deputy Ranger, the keeper at the lodge, remarkable for his civility, appears for your admission.'

The Princess married the Landgrave of Hesse in 1825, but continued as Ranger until 1835, Mrs. G.A. Bell, in a book called *Royal Manor of Richmond* written during the Victorian period, states that the Princess gave up her office in 1825, when it passed to the Landgravine of Hesse. Mrs. Bell had obviously *not* studied the history of the royal family of less than 50 years earlier!

In 1834, an area of about 100 acres was added to the park by the perseverance of Edward Jesse, the last Deputy Surveyor to the Commissioners of Woods, Forests and Land Revenues (who is thought to have died in a cottage in Sheen Lane near the East Sheen gate of the park). He purchased Sudbrook (or Petersham) Park from the estates of the Dysart family and incorporated it into the park. Today, a good view of the Petersham Park area can be seen from the gardens at the back of Pembroke Lodge.

In de Vere's *Handbook of Richmond Park*, he tells us in 1909 that 'this Petersham portion of the Park is reserved for the use of school fetes, bean feasts, etc., immense numbers of children and others going down every summer from London'.

In 1835, King William IV bestowed the Rangership on Adolphus Frederick, 1st Duke of Cambridge. This was confirmed by Queen Victoria, whose uncle he was, on 2 December 1837, during the first year of her reign. It was in 1848 that the first mention is made of the 'Commissioners of Works' undertaking work in the park. There was not a single Commissioner in charge at this time – he was not appointed until the beginning of the 20th century, but the Board of Works of George III's reign seems to have given place to a new organisation. It is very likely that most of the practical work of the upkeep of the park was now done by the Commissioners of Works, since the bestowing of the Rangership after George III gave it up became very much a 'grace and favour' appointment.

Early account and record books kept by Park Superintendents, and now in the possession of the Department of the Environment, give some interesting facts about the administration of the park during the second half of the 19th century and the money spent on it.

The estimate of labourers' wages for the month of April 1868, was £126 3s. 5d., while, for the same month in 1877, it had dropped to £91 16s. 1d. In those days, the Park Superintendent was also responsible for the upkeep of Richmond and Kew Roads and the amount estimated to be spent in April 1868, on the wages of labourers working on these roads was £40 9s. 6d. against £80 17s. 11d. – twice as much – for the same month in 1887. Park police were employed from about June 1868, and the *joint* weekly pay of four of them seems to have been £4 8s. 0d. at this time – and they were still earning the same joint pay in May 1877!

In April 1872, C. Johnson, H. Brown, John Stanard, John Jones, Thomas Jones and J. Brockwell were paid altogether £4 10s. 0d. for 'raking and burning leaves in Sudbrook Rough and mudding a pond there', while John Lane was paid 15s. for 'spudding thistles, etc.'. In May 1875, T. Nappin and T. Guntrip were paid £1 14s. 0d. for 'taking up and re-laying drains' in the park, while John Lane and James Fruin received the same sum for 'spudding thistles, etc.'. The labourers were regular– over a period of 11 years, their names appear in one account book again and again – but they were paid as casuals and not, apparently, taken on the permanent staff, although a note in another book on 19 March 1890, states 'The Treasury has decided that All Foremen and Labourers who entered the Service previous to April 1859, are entitled to pension'.

An interesting cross-section of some of the entries during 1894 states that General Clifton has been informed that 'the new gate at East Sheen Common shall be closed at sunset and that a park keeper be detailed off to preserve order' . . . the Clerk of Wandsworth District Board of Works has been informed that the water from the well at the Lodge [*which* lodge is not mentioned] is not used for drinking purposes and has not been so used for many years . . . that the Superintendent has been instructed to provide four more seats with backs at Kingston Gate . . . and that 'the Board [presumably "of Works"] accepted the offer of Richmond Corporation to water Park roads on the occasion of the Queen's visit to White Lodge'.

White Lodge has had a close association with the royal families throughout its existance. On the Duke of Cambridge's death in 1850, the Queen gave the Rangership to her aunt, Princess Mary, Duchess of Gloucester, who lived at White Lodge while she was Ranger. In 1858, the Prince of Wales (later King Edward VII) went to live there with his tutors and in1861, Queen Victoria with the Prince Consort spent a short time there after the death of her mother, the Duchess of Kent.

During 1867 and 1868, the Prince of Wales occasionally stayed there and in 1869 the Queen presented it to the Duke and Duchess of Teck. Their daughter, Princess Mary (later Queen Mary, wife of King George V) spent much of her girlhood there until her marriage in 1893 and returned there for a short time in 1894 when her eldest son, Edward, Prince of Wales (later King Edward VIII, now Duke of Windsor), was born there on 23 June.

Not only was the Prince of Wales the only child later to be a monarch to be born in Richmond Park, but there was another unusual feature attached to his birth at White Lodge. Never before had a child been born while his great-grandmother was occupying the British throne. Queen Victoria paid two visits to the park after the baby was born — one on 26 June to see the Duchess of York and her new great-grandson and a second on 16 July to

8. John Lewis, the brewer of Richmond, who re-established the right of the people of Richmond to a free passage through Richmond Park. The engraving, made by R. Field and published in 1793, is after an oil painting of Lewis by T. Stewart, which now hangs in Richmond Public Library *(Reproduced by courtesy of Richmond Libraries Committee)*

9. This print, which shows residents of Richmond asserting their right of way through the park by breaking down the wall, was published in 1751 after Princess Amelia had closed Richmond Park to the public. The parson in the picture is the Rev. Thomas Wakefield, the Richmond Anglican minister. *(Reproduced by courtesy of Richmond Libraries Committee)*

10. Old Lodge, which was demolished in the late 1830s. At the time this engraving was made, it was the residence of Philip Meadows, Esq. *(Reproduced by courtesy of Mr. L. Paton)*

11. White Lodge (then called New Lodge) as it looked when Viscount Sidmouth lived there at the beginning of the 19th century. *(Reproduced by courtesy of Mr. L. Paton)*

12. In the late 18th and early 19th centuries, admission of carriages to the park was still restricted. Owners had to show numbered season tickets to the gate keeper before they could be admitted. The illustration shows a ticket issued to Lord Mitford and signed by the Ranger, the Earl of Bute, during the 1770s. *(Reproduced by courtesy of Richmond Libraries Committee)*

13. Richmond Gate and Lodge from the outside during the 19th century *(Reproduced by courtesy of Mr. L. Paton)*

14 and 15. Sheen Lodge, once called the Dog Kennel, was occupied from 1852 until 1892 by Professor Sir Richard Owen, the first director of the Natural History Museum at South Kensington. *(Both reproduced by courtesy of Mr. L. Paton)*

attend the christening of Edward Albert Christian George Andrew Patrick David, which was performed at White Lodge by the Archbishop of Canterbury assisted by the Bishop of Rochester. And, probably to mark this extraordinary event, the Queen then conferred knighthoods on the Mayor of Richmond, Alderman J.W. Szlumper, and Mr. Frederick Wigan, the High Sheriff of Surrey.

The Duchess of Gloucester died in 1857 and the Queen next bestowed the Rangership on George, 2nd Duke of Cambridge, her first cousin.

The Duke of Cambridge was still Ranger when Queen Victoria died in 1901. *He* died in 1904, when her son, Edward VII, had ascended the throne for his short reign. Until the Duke's death, the King did nothing to alter the administrative situation in the park, in which he had always been most interested and in which he had spent a good deal of time.

Then Edward VII took over the duties of Ranger himself (as he did the Rangership of St. James's, Green and Hyde Parks), appointing a Deputy Ranger in each case. At the same time, he entrusted the complete care of the parks to the Commissioners of Works, discontinued the preservation of game in Richmond Park and threw open more than 100 acres of enclosure to the public which had previous been denied to them.

A 'minute' in the Office of Works' file from the first Commissioner of Works, Schomberg K. McDonnell, on 24 March 1904, records that 'Lord Knollys [the King's Private Secretary] in conversation today informed me that the King has decided to retain both these offices [the offices of Ranger of Richmond Park and of the three central parks] in his own hands; that His Majesty had also determined that the administrative work of the Parks in question should fall to the Office of Works in a greater degree than heretofore under His Majesty's personal supervision. That on the death or resignation of the present Deputy Ranger of Richmond Park, Rear-Admiral Sir A. Fitz-George, K.C.V.O., R.N., and of the Superintendent in the Department of the Ranger of St. James's, Green and Hyde Parks, Lt. Gen. R. Bateson, C.V.O., no further appointments to these positions should be made, but the King did not intend to disturb the present holders during their life time; that the warrants to appoint these two officers should be prepared in this office and sent to Lord Knollys for His Majesty's signature'. This statement was affirmed by the King on 27 March 1904, and signed by Lord Knollys.

In the draft warrants for the appointment of the two deputies in the files, it was stated that: 'The Commissioners of His Majesty's Works and Public Buildings will be charged with the general management of the said Park under the Park Regulations Act 1872.'

On 29 April 1904, the Commissioner of Works sent the two warrants for the King's signature to Lord Knollys at Buckingham Palace and there is a very illuminating note from the King himself, dated 1 May 1904, next to this letter in the file: 'I have signed the warrants but hope that the two Deputy Rangers fully understand that they can give no orders without my permission and any suggestions from them for the wellbeing of the Parks should be submitted to me through the First Commissioner of H.M. Works, etc.'.

The Ministry of Works' files also shed light on the working conditions and pay of some of the permanent members of the park's staff.

In March 1902, the Park Superintendent, Henry G. Sawyer, the third of his family to hold the position, asked to be allowed to retire on pension at the end of June, but, rather mysteriously, subsequently withdrew his request. At this time, Henry Sawyer was 61 and had been on the park's staff for nearly 30 years. Also combining the offices of head keeper and game keeper of the park, he was receiving a salary of £250 a year, plus £96 annually in lieu of fee. His assistant, Benjamin Wells, received a salary of £90 per annum.

A committee of enquiry five years earlier had reported that these emoluments were excessive and suggested that the Ranger should be invited to consider some reductions, but nothing had been done. In the same way that files of unsolved murder cases are never closed at police headquarters, many Government department files are left open if they contain unresolved points — and so this chance to economise on salaries was seized by the Office of Works, which suggested, in 1904, that both Mr. Sawyer and his assistant should retire on pension on 1 July (when Mr. Sawyer would have served 32 years), since, with the abolition of the preservation of game, their duties would cease to exist! There would, said this 'minute', 'be no difficulty in arranging that the Board's officers should discharge his duties and those of the deputy superintendent'.

Mr. Sawyer *was* retired on 1 July 1904, but his assistant stayed on in the same position. He was given £10 a year more, which was to rise annually by £5 to £125, working under S. Pullman, who was made Superintendent, at a salary of £175, rising by £7 10s. 0d. annually to £225, instead of his previous salary as 'foreman' of £143 a year. He was also to have 'a residence and the run of two cows as at present'. Mr. Wells was to have the same.

During this re-arrangement, which did not, as today, carry with it redundancy pay for those who lost their jobs, the Office of Works sacked one keeper and three underkeepers. The changes made an immediate saving of £413 per year and, said the notes, an ultimate saving of £338 per year. But giving with one hand and taking with the other as public bodies are wont to do, the Office of Works added this warning: 'in view of the increased area to be made available to the public, an increased expenditure upon maintenance may have to be incurred.'

In fact, Admiral Fitz-George outlived the King by 12 years and, when he died in 1922, the post of Deputy Ranger was allowed to lapse. However, in 1932, it was revived for Sir Louis Greig, at the special wish of King George V. Sir Louis and his family lived at Thatched House Lodge until his death in 1953 and, although he wished his son to succeed him as Deputy Ranger, no further appointment was made and the office has now completely and finally lapsed, as did the office of Ranger after the death of King Edward VII.

During the two World Wars, the Army was stationed in the park. In the 1914–18 war, the park was used as a training ground for, among others, the London Grey Brigade (composed of the London Scottish, Artists' Rifles, Queen's Westminsters and Queen Victoria's Rifles). During the 1939–45 war, it was used by the anti-aircraft section and there were ammunition dumps and an

A.T.S. camp there.

After World War II, the Office of Works became the Ministry of Works and, in 1963, when it took over responsibility for building work for the Armed Forces, it became the Ministry of Public Building and Works, which, in 1970, became part of the Department of the Environment. Throughout these changes and to the present day, the Parks Directorate, which started in the Office of Works, continued and it has always looked after Richmond Park, as it has London's other Royal Parks.

Though White Lodge has been dealt with earlier in this book, no history of Richmond Park would be complete without a few words about some of the other important residences in it.

Pembroke Lodge, between Richmond and Ham Gates, which started as the Molecatcher's Cottage and was later called Hill Lodge, was renamed Pembroke Lodge probably when Elizabeth, Countess of Pembroke lived there. She was the widow of the 10th Earl of Pembroke, who is said to have built the original Stone Lodge (later White Lodge) for George II, and was one of the reigning beauties at the court of George III, who occasionally visited her at Pembroke Lodge. The Countess died there in 1831 at the age of 93. The original Molecatcher's Cottage was, by that time, only a very small part of the house which had been extended on both sides of it.

A charmingly stilted Victorian publication published in 1851 and called *A Guide or Handbook to Richmond New Park in three Languages, English, French and German* (probably one of the first English guide books to be published in more than one language), describes Pembroke Lodge as 'formerly known as Virmin [sic] Killers' Lodge'! The writer of it says of the Dowager Countess of Pembroke: '... but personal attraction was not alone her endowment, for she possessed in a large degree that most excellent gift, a truly charitable mind.'

In 1788, Sir John Soane, the architect, was asked to make alterations and additions to the 'cottage' in Richmond New Park belonging to Lady Pembroke. Drawings in Sir John Soane's Museum correspond fairly closely with the exterior of Pembroke Lodge as it is today, but there is little left now of the interior additions and alterations that Soane made.

Among the suggested additions he proposed was a kitchen wing, but it is unlikely that the final alterations were those he suggested. Also in Sir John Soane's Museum is a design for a kitchen wing dated 1792 and Miss Dorothy Stroud believes it may be a suggestion by Henry Holland for what he considered was an improvement on one of Soane's designs. Soane was very angry about this and the plan was probably the cause of a bitter letter from him to Lady Pembroke protesting that she had submitted his last plans to 'Mr. Holland the Builder.' On the drawing itself, the enraged architect has pencilled many satirical notes, such as 'corridor — the straights of Thermophylae' and 'servants hall — floored en parquetage'!

Eventually, the architect seems to have recovered from his indignation and not only carried out several other alterations for Lady Pembroke at Pembroke Lodge during 1796 (by which time he had been appointed Deputy Surveyor of Woods and Forests), but also at her house in Charles Street, Berkeley Square, London.

After the Countess of Pembroke's death, Pembroke Lodge was occupied by the Earl of Errol who had married Elizabeth Fitzclarence, one of the daughters of King William IV by the actress, Mrs. Jordon. The King used to visit his daughter there and the *Victoria County History* records that, on 10 September 1832, he received an address there from the people of Richmond.

The Earl died in 1846 and the lodge was granted by Queen Victoria in 1847 to her Prime Minister, Lord John (Earl) Russell, who died there in 1878. His grandson, the philosopher Bertrand Russell (who became the 3rd Earl), spent most of his childhood and early youth there, leaving Pembroke Lodge to go to university when he was about 20. His grandmother stayed on until her death in 1898. Her daughter, Lady Agatha Russell, lived in the house after she died and, when she left it, Georgina Elizabeth, Countess of Dudley, occupied it until *her* death in 1929.

It is thought that Thatched House Lodge was either an old building improved, or an entirely new building erected, by Sir Robert Walpole, who is said to have spent a great deal of money on it. There had either been two earlier buildings on the site or one which had been renamed during its existence. In a Treasury

Paper dated 3 September 1716, there is an item of £40 for 'repairing Aldrich's Lodge.' Charles Aldridge, undoubtedly a park keeper, died on 7 January 1736, when he was 59, and was buried in Petersham churchyard. In Eyre's map of 1754 (discussed in the next chapter), there is an 'Aldridge's Lodge' on the site of Thatched House Lodge. In later maps and references, it is called Burkitt's, Burchett's, Burcher's or Burches Lodge. John Burkitt or Burchett, also a keeper, died there in 1796, aged 77, and was buried near his predecessor at Petersham.

Certainly by 1813, the name had been changed to Thatched House Lodge — it was noted on a plan of that year, (also discussed in the next chapter). In its grounds there is still a thatched ice house (or summer house), the ceilings and walls of which are covered with paintings attributed to Angelica Kauffman (circa 1780), and this may have been the reason for the Lodge's name.

Sir John Soane, in his official capacity of Deputy Surveyor of Woods and Forests, made some alterations there in 1798 when the house was occupied by General Sir Charles Stuart. Although some more changes were made at the beginning of the 20th century, much of what is left corresponds to Sir John Soane's plans.

General Sir Edward Bowater, a Copenhagen, Peninsular War and Waterloo veteran and equerry to the Prince Consort, lived there from about 1841 until he died there in 1861. His widow lived on at the Lodge until her death in October 1904. Sir Frederick Treves, the eminent surgeon, lived there from 1907 until 1919. Sir Louis Greig, as previously noted, occupied it when he was Deputy Ranger and his widow and son were granted a new lease for three years after his death, leaving it in 1956. The tenant immediately before Princess Alexandra and the Hon. Angus Ogilvy and their family, who live there today, was the Duke of Sutherland.

Sheen Lodge, once a keeper's lodge called the Dog Kennel, and later Sheen Cottage, was granted by George III to the Scottish Baron William Adam of Blair Adam, Lord High Commissioner of Scotland, whose name is perpetuated in Adam's Pond, near Sheen Gate. The first Director of the Natural History

Museum at South Kensington, Professor Sir Richard Owen, lived at Sheen Lodge for 40 years — from 1852 until 1892 — and he had a private gate out of the park from his house. He entertained many famous people there, including Charles Dickens, the painter Sir John Millais and Queen Victoria's Prime Minister, William Ewart Gladstone.

V

THE CHANGING FACE

THE AREA of the park and its boundaries have remained virtually unchanged since Charles I enclosed it except for the inclusion of Petersham Park in 1834, but what is *inside* the park has changed very considerably. The surprisingly large number of maps and plans of it still in existence illustrate this very clearly.

An enclosure map was made for Charles I in 1637, but an earlier map or plan of the proposed park also exists and can be seen in the London Museum. It was made about 1635, presumably also for the King's use. It shows how much of Mortlake Parish would be taken to make the park, but is so roughly drawn that it seems to indicate that most of the proposed enclosure was common land — the 'comons' of Richmond, Petersham, Mortlake, Ham, Kingston and Putney are shown, as are also Beverley Plaine and Blacke Heathe, but no private person's land is indicated.

Two years later, the 1637/8 enclosure map was much more detailed and indicated clearly that almost half the park had belonged to private owners. It is true that, on the Richmond side, the Warren and Berry Grove were Crown lands, but, just above them, a Mr. Cole and a John Garnett had their lands. To the right of Mortlake and Richmond Commons, a large tract had been owned by a number of people — Humfrey Bennett, Henrie White, Guy Holdsworth, a Mr. Wilkes and a Mr. Juckes. Cutting round Mortlake Common was a good deal more of Mr. Juckes's land and, below Mortlake Common and extending right to the boundaries of the park between what are now Sheen and Roehampton Gates, was a mass of private lands, a good deal owned by Humfrey Bennett, some by John Cole Esqre, some by Mr. White and Mr. Olley, both of Putney, Mr. Mussey, William Lodge and some more owned by a Mr. Gillin.

Abutting the 'rode way from Kingston to London' on

Combe Pars, Mr. John Cole had lived at Gibbet Close and on the other side of Blacke Heath in the Kingston corner of the park, Robert Harrison, Gent, had had a big estate called Lambert Hawes; William Chitton had had *his* estate divided in half by the park's high wall, as had Mr. Nabler and Mr. Knightly. John Price and two other small landowners had had to sell their estates to the King. There may well, in addition, have been a number of other small landowners whom the map does not indicate.

Just outside the wall that enclosed Richmond Common, a windmill is shown, but Henry VII's Tudor Palace nearby is not, though it appears on later maps. Pale Common is shown on this map, too, near where Palewell Common is today.

This then, was how the park looked just after its enclosure. If the map (which is in the Public Record Office in remarkably good condition) is to be believed, there were quite a few trees, much open land, some of it farm land, and no ponds or other stretches of water except two streams running across the centre of the park and what is probably the present Beverley Brook running across Beverley Plain and along the borders of Roehampton.

Also in the Public Record Office is a map made by Elias Allen about the same time as the 'official' enclosure map, of which unfortunately only about two thirds survives. This map *does* indicate Richmond Palace, in Richmond Town itself, but not very far away from the park wall. The spelling of some of the names on it, such as Mourtlacke, leads one to suppose it is slightly earlier than the two foregoing, although it may just have been the diversity of spelling of those days.

But the names of the commons did seem to differ from map to map. The John Rocque Survey of London indicated Pestilent Common (now gone) and East Sheen Common for the first time. Also for the first time, we find Oliver's Mound, believed to have been associated with Oliver Cromwell who is supposed to have stood there on occasion during the years of the Commonwealth.

The most significant change in the two maps with just over a hundred years between them is that in the 1741—45 Rocque map the first indication of what are now Pen Ponds is shown. Man-made and known in the 19th century as The Canals, the two stretches of water, separated only by a path, are obviously fed by the three streams (one with a tributary) shown on the map. As was noted in the last chapter, it is believed that Princess Amelia had the ponds constructed from gravel pits when she was Ranger, but since she did not take up office until 1751 and the Rocque maps were made at least six years earlier, she could not have actually created the ponds. It is much more likely that she merely had their shape altered slightly and re-named them!

Coopers Lodge has been built and another big building is indicated fairly near the Canals. This is Old Lodge (probably the original Hartleton Farm), which fell into poor condition in the 1780s and was pulled down some time between 1839 and 1841. White Lodge (then called New Lodge, to distinguish it from the Old Lodge), built by George II, is also shown.

In fact, an astonishing amount of work had been done and changes made in the park in a hundred years. If the map is accurate, many of the old buildings had been swept away, plant-ations had been formed and the three big houses mentioned above had been built. None of the streams flowing into the Canals were noted on earlier maps, while the streams that *were* noted, one possibly a spring, seem to have been absorbed by the Canals and the outflow of the old stream into Beverley Brook seems to have completely disappeared.

The appreciation of landscaping in the park is clearly shown on this map, by the formation of the paths in front of Old Lodge, which provided a triangle of grassland before it, and a path straight down from the point of the triangle of the grassland and between the Canals, giving a beautiful view. It is further indicated by the planting of the tree plantations to form the Queen's Ride (which is still there today) in front of White (or New) Lodge.

Two maps exist for the year 1754, both prepared in the month of September, one by Edward John Eyre, Surveyor, and a far less detailed version, cartographer un-named, for Princess Amelia in the fourth year of her Rangership.

On the first of the two maps, we can see, even more clearly than on the 1741/45 map, the great changes and additions that had taken place. Now all the gates of the park are shown — some with slightly different names from today. The carriage gates are Richmond Hill Gate, Ham Gate, Kingston Comon Gate, Robin Hood Gate, Roehampton Gate and East Sheen Gate. Then there is Chohole Gate and bridle gate, leading to Putney Heath (probably a foot gate), which is now gone, a gate marked 'late Combe Gate now a bridle gate' near Kingston Comon Gate and, next to it, another bridle gate. Also shown is a bridle gate near Pestilent Common and, above the East Sheen Common area of the park, Bog Gate.

In addition to what are now Pen Ponds (for the first time on a map or plan called 'The Canals'), ponds are to be found in the grounds of Old Lodge (which now has a wide lawn in front of it), near Roehampton Gate, at the Putney Heath end of the park and near Bog Gate. A reservoir is indicated fairly near the Canals with a springhead above it and another springhead is found near Kingston Comon Gate. A bridge has been built over Beverley Brook near Robin Hood Gate and a large triangular area at the Putney Heath corner, with a farm house shown in it, is now called The Paddock, where deer and farm animals may have been kept. Molecatcher's Cottage is shown between Richmond Hill and Kingston Comon gates, with a well near it. Above it is the Henry VIII Mound on which legend has it the King stood on 19 May 1536, when he was brought the news, while out hunting, of Queen Anne Boleyn's execution.

Agnes Strickland, in her book *Lives of the Queens of England*, written in the 19th century, describes the occasion almost as if she was there! 'On the morning of the 19th May, 1536, Henry VIII, clad for the chase with his huntsmen and hounds round him, was standing breathless on a mound in Richmond Park, awaiting the signal-gun from the Tower which was to announce that the sword had fallen on the neck of his once entirely loved Anne Boleyn. At last, when the bright sun rose high towards the meridian, the sullen sound of the death-gun boomed along the winding of the Thames. Henry started with ferocious joy. "Ha! ha!" he cried with satisfaction. "The deed is done! Uncouple the hounds and away!" '

Jane Seymour, it is said, was waiting in the Richmond House of Sir George and Lady Carew for the news of her predecessor's end to free King Henry to marry her — which he did eight days later — so it is possible that Henry was waiting for the news near at hand in order to let her know as soon as possible. It is *possible,* but since there is strong historical evidence that the King spent the evening of his wife's execution at a revel at Wolfe Hall, Wiltshire — some 60 miles away from Richmond — it is doubtful that even a horseman as good as Henry VIII could have covered that distance in about six hours!

Then again, the Tower of London is nearly 11 miles from the mound and many different versions of the signal exist. Some writers say that it was the sound of a gun, others the flash of a gun ... a black flag ... a rocket! As H.M. Cundall points out in his book *Bygone Richmond,* '... it is a question whether at that distance it would be possible to see the flash or to hear the sound of a gun of that period, or even to observe the bursting of a rocket at noon time in the month of May; to say nothing of being able to discern a black flag.'

On the 1637 enclosure map, this mound is marked 'The King's Standinge' and it is far more likely that this refers to Charles I and not his Tudor ancestor. The spot is on the highest ground in the park and it could have been where the King — or his representatives — stood to issue orders when surveying the land before the enclosure. It is also possible that the mound was the King's standing place for shooting deer as they were driven past him in the open space in front.

Despite all this reasoned conjecture, however, the name which appears in the 1754 map has stuck and the legend, probably because of its rather sinister romance, persists.

Very near Richmond Hill Gates there is a 'summer house.' Fairly near the reservoir, White Ash Lodge has appeared and Aldridge's Lodge is found near the lower springhead. For the first time, 'Dog Kennell' is shown on the Palewell Common (now called 'Palewell' instead of 'Pale') side. This was a dwelling, built in the first place for a keeper or bailiff, which later became Sheen Cottage and finally Sheen Lodge.

The owners of the land immediately outside the Kingston-Richmond side of the park have changed. Two big estates are owned by the Duchess of Argyle (nearer to Kingston) and the Earl of Harrington.

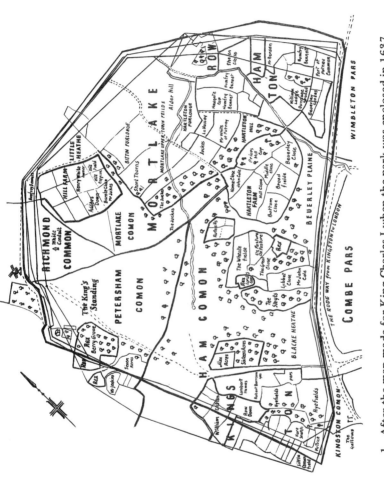

1. After the map made for King Charles I when the park was enclosed in 1637
(*Reproduced by courtesy of the Public Record Office*)

2. From the 'Survey of London', 1746, by John Rocque

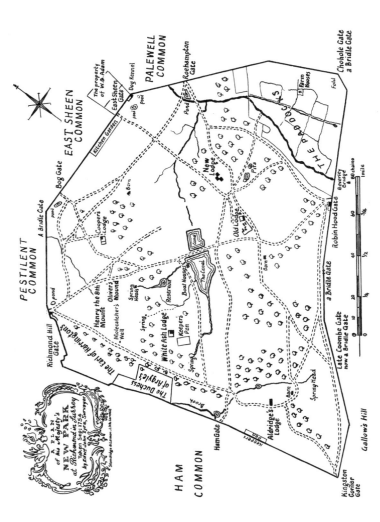

3. After the map made for King George II by Edward John Eyre, Surveyor, in the fourth year of the Rangership of his daughter, Princess Amelia. A similar map made by Eyre for Princess Amelia herself is privately owned.

(Reproduced by courtesy of the Public Record Office)

4. A guide plan made in 1876 for the 6d. book *A History of Richmond New Park*

The map made for Princess Amelia differs only on one important point. The shape of the Canals is shown to be different from those in any of the earlier maps including the contemporary one. Now they begin to assume the proportions of the Pen Ponds of today. The larger of them comes to a point on the Richmond-Kingston side and though the changes may be man-made, silting up may also have played a part in the changed shape. Near the Dog Kennel, another pond is shown and to the left of East Sheen Gate, a Garden House and Kitchen is indicated.

Less than 20 years later, in 1771, another plan was prepared by Thomas Richardson on the orders of His Majesty's Surveyor General, T. Burrett. Again, there are many changes, though not so drastic as the earlier ones. The word 'Hill' has been dropped from Richmond Gate and 'Comon' from Kingston Gate and Chohole Gate has disappeared. Pestilent Common has become Pest House Common and Bog Gate, near East Sheen Common, is now called the Queen's Private Gate. Near it, another paddock has been built. Now, oddly enough, shown just *inside* the park, though the Earl of Harrington still owns his estate, the Duchess of Argyle has apparently sold hers to Lady Greenwich and, outside the wall between Roehampton and Putney, the Earl Bessborough now has a large estate.

Near Kingston Gate, Thatched House Plain is indicated, but not the lodge of the same name, and, below it, the gate there is called 'Coombe Gate' again. Black Heath (omitted from the two 1754 maps) is shown and, above it, we see the first indication of Isabell Slade (probably meaning glade or wood). White Ash Wood now surrounds White Ash Lodge, Pond Slade is placed near the Canals which, strangely enough, are *not* indicated and the top end of the Queen's Ride is surrounded by Lucas's Wood (probably called after the first Park Superintendent, John Lucas).

Two years before the Battle of Waterloo, in 1813, another plan was made. The last 21 years of this 42-year period, George III was Ranger and, although he did not carry out all his plans, considerable changes, some of which he must have made, can be seen. The total area of the park is given on this plan as 2,253 acres, one rod, three poles; very little different from today and, considering that in those days measurements were not so accurate, probably nearly the same dimensions.

Near Ham Gate, we see Thatched House Lodge on the plain of the same name for the first time, with another paddock on the Ham Common boundary above it. Lucay's [sic] Lodge is to be found above and to the right of Lucas's Wood (now not indicated by name) and near a new hay barn and feeding place — there are several of them round the park.

In the grounds of the Old Lodge, an enclosure marks 'King Tree', but I can find no reference to the reason for it. The area in the Putney corner called 'The Paddocks' in the 1754 and 1771 maps is now divided into fields, each one carefully named. The one on the far corner is, interestingly enough, called 'Chohole'. The bridle gate near Pest House Common is now called Pesthouse Gate and the Queen's Private Gate is now also called Bog Gate. Isabell Slade has become Isabella Slade.

The next plan that tells us anything about the park is an 1851 hand-drawn tithe map by E. & G. Driver of 5, Whitehall, which can be found in the Surrey Record Office. It is of that part of the park in the Parishes of Putney and Mortlake. This does not, alas, indicate the changes that must have taken place in 38 years, but it does show that all the tithes payable for the park were to go to the Dean and Chapter of Worcester. In all, about 30 tithe-bound acres in the park provided an annual payment of £4. 19s. 0d.

The next plan is a small one made in 1876 as a 'guide plan' in an intriguing little book, *A History of Richmond New Park* by a Resident, already mentioned. The writer is now thought to have been either one of the Lucas family employed in the park or someone closely connected with them.

Although this map is on a very small scale, great changes can still be seen. Though the main carriage gates remain unchanged, the foot gates are more numerous, though some of them are private gates. Among the private gates, Chohole has appeared again. Professor Owen has his own gate from Sheen Lodge. The kitchen garden gate is private, as is the Queen's Gate, the Pest House Gate and a nearby Keeper's gate. Petersham Gate (apparently a right of way) has appeared by Countess Russell's School, which is actually in the Park fairly near Richmond Gate. All traces of the school have disappeared today and no records of the pupils or its duration seem to exist, though since Countess Russell lived on at Pembroke Lodge for 20 years after her husband died in 1878, it seems likely that the school was probably started by her in the early 1880s.

Coombe Gate has had its name changed to Ladder Style Gate, probably as a result of John Lewis's law suit against Princess Amelia.

One of the most interesting changes is that the Canals are now merely called lakes (with Ponds Game Preserve above them) and a small pond some way from them, but served by a stream flowing from them, is called Pen Pond! It is true, however, that it is near a deer pen which tempers one's first reaction that it is a mistake.

Sidmouth Wood is now a game preserve, as is Isabella Slade –now called Isabell again–and Spankers Hill Preserve has appeared in what was probably some of the grounds of the Old Lodge which has now gone.

Behind White Lodge is Box Tree Wood and Broomfield Hill lies near the Isabell Game Preserve. Near Pest House Gate are paddocks and the Conduit Game Preserve and, near it and the Head Keeper's House, the Inns of Court Drill Ground — so Richmond Park had once again been host to the Army!

On a map of the park drawn specially for his book by Coryn de Vere in 1909, the park begins to look much more as we know it today.

Pen Ponds, only slightly different in shape, have assumed or re-assumed the name that Princess Amelia is said to have given them, while the first pond called Pen Pond has become Leg of Mutton Pond, as it still is. There is no longer preservation of game, so the game preserves have all become woods or plantations, including Isabella, which is shown as being *in* Isabella Slade for the first time. A cricket ground has appeared near the Queen's Pond at Kingston Gate. Holly Lodge, later to be called Bog Lodge, is seen near Bog Gate and, below it, and nearer to Kingston Gate lies Sawyer's Hill, called undoubtedly after the Sawyer family who served the park so well.

The Duke of Fife now lives at East Sheen, just outside East Sheen Gate, and this association is perpetuated in the Fife Road of today, which runs right across the top of Sheen Lane where it meets the park gates.

Again there are many changes. The park is far more a public place, though there are still prohibited areas. Nevertheless, social awareness is creeping in, for a public walk is indicated from Richmond Workhouse just outside the park wall (by the cemetary and between Richmond and Bog Gates) across a rifle club range. It is strange that the workhouse has not been shown in earlier maps, since, in E. Beresford Chancellor's *History and Antiquities of Richmond, Kew, Petersham and Ham* published in 1894, he explains that it was originally erected in 1786 by George III 'who gave it with the surrounding 32 acres to the Parish in compensation for having enclosed the road known as Love Lane between Kew and Richmond'. The boundary, he says, was enlarged in 1836 for 'the purpose of the union under the 'new poor law' which includes the parishes of Richmond, Petersham, Kew, Mortlake and Barnes'. It was enlarged again in the 1890s.

The latest map was produced by the Ordnance Survey for the Ministry of Public Building and Works in 1962. Laid over it with red lines and old English printing is a version of the 1637 enclosure map, so that the reader can see at a glance the changes that 300 years have wrought in the park.

VI

FLORA AND FAUNA

RICHMOND PARK has become as famous for its animal and plant life as for its human inhabitants. And the development of its flora and fauna has had almost as much effect on its history as the deeds and misdeeds of those humans who have been closely associated with it.

The Deer

There is no doubt that for most people the park's greatest attraction is the Queen's deer — the herds of large red deer and dainty, dappled fallow deer which roam freely over the park's acres.

There were deer on the site of Richmond Park long before Henry VIII hunted there at Shene Chase. The numbers have fluctuated over the years (probably both because of hunting and disease) since the enclosure, when there were about 1,500 animals. From 1656-1658, there were still about 1,500—1,300 fallow and 200 red deer. By 1660, State Papers record that there were 2,000, but in the following nine years the number had dropped to only 600. For nearly 200 years, there is no record, but, in 1834, there were 1,600 fallow deer and between 40 and 50 red deer. This number stayed fairly constant until 1886, when a contemparary writer, R. Crisp, reports that the fallow deer were reduced by more than 100. The number dropped again 10 years later to 1,300 fallow deer and a 'small herd' of red deer, but, in 1883, there were 1,500 deer in all.

In 1892, there were between 1,100 and 1,200 fallow and 50 red deer. By 1909, the numbers of the fallow had fallen drastically to 900. In 1937, there were only 300 fallow and 80 red deer. Today, there are about 600 deer in the park—350 fallow and 250 red deer.

From fairly soon after the enclosure until the beginning of the 20th century, deer were given winter feeding and shelter in enclosed paddocks. In 1909, there were still six deer folds or pens in the park. After King Edward VII became Ranger in 1904, he did away with the deer folds when he discontinued the preservation of game in the park and, from that time, the deer have had free range, since it is considered they are healthiest in these conditions.

Over the years, the health of the deer herds seems to have been fairly good, as it is today – with one notable exception. In the year 1886 (when Crisp tells us the fallow deer were reduced by 100), they fell prey to an outbreak of rabies, according to an official report issued by Mr. A. Cope, Chief Inspector of the Agricultural Department of the Privy Council Office and Professor Victor Horsley, Professor Superintendent of the Brown Institution of Wandsworth Bridge Road, London, S.W.

'The first indication of the incidence of any disease among the deer was the discovery by the keepers towards the end of September, 1886, of a doe, which was suckling a fawn, staggering about in her pasturing near the entrance gate at East Sheen,' states the report. The keepers killed the doe and they found that much of the hair was rubbed off its head. A few days later, keepers noticed other deer behaving in the same manner: 'biting the skin of their shoulders and bellies until they were practically raw, tearing out their hair and, at times, they charged other deer'.

The keepers also noticed that, as a rule, the animals appeared to feed up to the time of their death and when the contents of their stomachs were examined afterwards, pieces of stick and other things which the deer would normally refuse as food were found. All the animals stricken with the disease showed the same symptoms, some becoming very violent before they died, which was usually 2-3 days after they were first seen to be unwell.

By April 1887, 160 deer had died – all, says the report, 'presenting decided symptoms of some form of nervous disease which, in many instances, ended in paralysis and always in the death of the animal'.

In June 1887, the epidemic broke out again and continued

until 24 September, by which time 264 animals had died. Research and experiments confirmed that the disease was definitely rabies and it was assumed that one or more stray dogs which had got into the park had, when infectious, bitten the deer and so started off the epidemic. I can find no other such reports before or since the 1886-7 publication, but it is possible that a similar outbreak may have been the cause of the sharp drop, which is noted above, from 2,000 to 600 between 1660 and 1669.

The Trees

The varied and profuse English trees in the park are an unforgettable sight at all times of the year. Throughout the park's long history, those caring for it, particularly recent Superintendents, have concentrated on both keeping the specifically 'English' character of the trees and carefully planning for the future by sensible and consistant felling of old trees and the regular planting of seedlings of many kinds to replace them in the most natural fashion.

Some of the trees still in the park today, particularly oaks, were certainly growing at the enclosure and many more are at least 200 years old. From the start, the park was well furnished with trees, among which oaks predominated, but, during the hundred years following the enclosure, there are references to felling but none to planting. It is more than likely that very little planned planting was carried out before George III, who started planning on a large scale during his reign. Lord Sidmouth, who was appointed Deputy Ranger in 1813, began the systematic establishment of plantations and added more than 20. This policy continued, with one break of about 20 years, throughout the century — and, in 1824, a nursery for oak trees was also started.

In 1834, when Petersham Park was added to Richmond Park, the fence and trees dividing the two were removed and a terrace walk of beech was planted from Richmond Gate to Poet's Corner in the Petersham Park area, and the Hornbeam Walk, which follows the old boundary southward from Pembroke

Lodge, may have been planted as a continuation of this avenue.

Right up to the end of the 19th century, 'maintenance planting' as well as the setting up of new plantations was continued. The policy was to plant groups and isolated trees with only occasional plantations and, at the turn of the century, the establishment of new plantations seems to have ceased, except for 'ceremonial' plantings, which had started towards the end of the 19th century to commemorate Royal occasions by planting small plantations. The first of these commemorates Queen Victoria's 1887 Jubilee and there have been a number since, the most recent being the Coronation Plantation of 1953.

It is estimated that there are about 200,000 trees in the park today. With oak predominating, they also include English Elm, Wych Elm, Common Beech, Hornbeam, Spanish and Horse Chestnut, Willow, Sycamore and some Ash. Very few conifers are grown in the park, but some very fine Cedars of Lebanon can be found in the Petersham Park area, as well as two other species of Cedar — the Deodar and the Atlantica. Among the most prevelant berry-bearing species are the Common Thorn, the Rowan or Mountain Ash and the Whitebeam.

A tree which is remembered only because of its rather evil reputation is the Old Shrew Ash which has now disappeared though it was still just standing— carefully propped up – in the early 1930s. Situated just to the south of Adam's Pond near Sheen Gate, it was reputed to be more than 300 years old and was made a 'shrew' ash by having a hole bored in its trunk and a live shrew mouse inserted and securely plugged in, because it was supposed to have a baneful effect on other animals. The Shrew Ash was later thought to cure ailing children and, for many years, mothers took their sick children to the tree and passed them nine times under and over a bar set in the trunk, with suitable incantations!

Many trees in the park have been struck by lightning over the generations — and this is not uncommon today. As early as 1711, on 20 May, the historian Aubrey records the destruction of trees by lightning. On 6 August 1885, when two oak trees near White Lodge were shattered in a thunder storm which had hit Richmond about three o'clock in the afternoon, the effect was so bizarre as to provoke a long and involved description of what happened in an article by John T. Beighton in 1887 in a magazine called *Leisure Hours.*

'The trees' Mr. Beighton explains 'were about 70 feet high and the growth of one, at 3 feet from the roots, was 11 feet and the other 12 feet and the distance between them about 23 feet. They stood about 100 feet above sea level, the highest part of the park being 184. They were in a group of oaks at the western side of Queen's Ride.'

'In the case of one of them, the effect was the ordinary one when lightning seizes a tree. It was struck near its summit, tearing away the broad branches and heaving them to the ground, but damaging the bark in the way the trunk is split.'

'The effect on the other tree was extraordinary and probably unique. The tree was struck about 30 feet from the ground and it cut through the trunk so as to throw to the ground in one mass some 40 feet of the tree, with the bark unimpaired, and the current, at the same time, rushed downwards rending the trunk asunder in such fragments, flinging the unburnt and even unscorched bark in tiny shreds to great distances around, and then penetrating the ground at the root and pulverising the soil embedding itself in the earth. Some of the gigantic splinters were solid, others torn into strips. Some of them, several inches thick and 10-15 feet long, stood up and spread out like a gigantic fan, gripping amongst them branches which fell from the upper part of the tree.'

'There was one piece of timber weighing apparently about a cwt, lying 120 feet from the tree! The first effect of the strike' Mr. Beighton concludes, 'was like that of a giant's scimitar horizontally cutting through the tree and the next that of a stupendous bombshell exploding within the remainder of the trunk. All this must have been accomplished in a few seconds.'

The Plantations and Woods

There are today a number of plantations and woods in the park, most of them the game reserves of pre-1904 days and many of them now open to the public. The plantations are named Pond,

Queen Elizabeth, George V, Jubilee, Kingston Hill, Saw Pit, White Lodge, Lawn, Tercentenary, Hamcross, Teck, Isabella and Coronation. By far the biggest of the numerous woods are Sidmouth, now a closed bird sanctuary, and the 25-acre Spankers Hill, which is open to the public.

Of the plantations, the most important and beautiful is undoubtedly the Isabella Plantation or Garden and much of the credit for this is due to Park Superintendent George Thomson, who retired in 1971. When Mr. Thomson—a Scottish tree expert who was, for some years, with the Forestry Commission—was appointed Superintendent in 1951, the 42-acre plantation was no more than a charming woodland. Today, thanks to his planning and the work of his staff, most of it is an enchanted garden with a wide and fascinating collection of flowering shrubs, such as Rhododendron, Azalea, Camelia, Magnolia and Heather, and a running brook, artificially diverted, edged with waterside plants of many kinds.

There are several ponds, one named after the Superintendent himself, and planned vistas with tree-trunk seats from which to enjoy them. For the autumn colours, there are carefully selected and placed trees and shrubs to take over, with their varied hues, when the flowering shrubs have done.

The Isabella Plantation is at its most colourful in late April and early May and this is the time when thousands of people, many with their dogs (on leads), come to see it.

The Birds

The Park is home to thousands of birds. In 1970, a hundred different species, 52 of them breeding species, were officially recorded by the Committee on Bird Sanctuaries in the Royal Parks. Figures for the three preceding years were: 1967, 97 species (50 breeding); 1968, 92 species (55 breeding); and 1969, 96 species (53 breeding). It seems that the number of birds has not fluctuated very much over the last few years, though there is a sharp drop from about 35 years ago when, in 1937, C.L. Collenette, the park's official bird observer at that time, recorded no fewer than 132 different species of birds in the park, 46 of them residents, i.e., birds which usually breed and some of which remain throughout the year.

There must be many reasons for the reduction of species of birds in the park over the years — possibly one of the most important is that, with the fairly fast urban building programme abutting the park, the shyer birds tend to stay away. There is no doubt, however, that, with more people bringing more food especially in the winter time, the indigenous birds have flocked in greater numbers, as can be seen if one stands quietly by the 'bird' tree stump in the Isabella Plantation after some breadcrumbs have been dropped on it.

Another important reason, for some species disappearing —and in the 1930s Collenette was also worried about this—is that quite a number of them are dependent on the withered bracken of the previous year as ground cover in which to nest 'and the most harmful effect on the birds of the number of people and horsemen who now use the park is the beating down and flattening of this withered bracken, which greatly reduces the nesting areas'.

But many interesting birds were seen in the park during 1969 and 1970, the latest recorded periods. A number of unusual aquatic birds were seen at Pen Ponds, for instance. On one day in March 1969, an observer, standing in the Alder Spinney by the upper pond, saw a Red-necked Grebe, a very rare visitor, and a Goosander within a few yards of one another and, in the trees within easy range, a Treecreeper, Goldfinches and some Siskins. Goosanders appeared on several occasions during 1970 and, in both years, a pair of Great Crested Grebes nested successfully on both ponds, each rearing one young— and single Little Grebes were seen on several occasions.

Mallard, says the official report, which breed in the old oaks in the park, were always present in good numbers, with a few Tufted Ducks and Pochards — the latter definitely breeding. Occasionally, they were joined, for short periods, by casual visitors such as the Teal, Gadwall and Wigeon, and a Shoveler and a Goldeneye were seen on single occasions, while the wild, rare Red-necked Grebe stayed for about three weeks.

The ponds also attracted large numbers of gulls during the

autumn and winter. Black Headed Gulls predominated and there were many Herring Gulls, some Common Gulls and a few Lesser Black-backs. An occasional migrating Tern was seen - a Black Tern in May 1969, and a Sandwich Tern the following September. A Heron was quite often seen in both years and two Cormorants were observed flying over in March 1970. Mute Swans and Canada Geese, neither of which bred successfully, were also present.

Among the birds of prey, a remarkable number of Kestrels were seen in the park. 20 pairs bred in 1969 and slightly fewer in 1970. A Montagu Harrier was observed only once – on 11 October 1969.

Often to be seen were Pheasants and Partridges, which bred regularly, and Water Rail during the winter. Small parties of Lapwing often flew over but, says the report, they are more disturbed by the greater occupation of the park than they used to be. Woodcock could be seen constantly in the plantations, where they probably breed. Snipe and, very occasionally, Jack Snipe were flushed from time to time and other waders, such as the Common Sandpiper and the Green Sandpiper, were seen.

Wood-pigeons come in their thousands at acorn time. One pair of Stock Doves was seen and three Turtle Doves.

The distinctive call of that most British of avian interlopers, the Cuckoo, was heard regularly during the same two years. The Barn Owl bred again, three or four pairs of Tawny Owls and the Little Owl were seen and probably bred and a very rare species, the Short-eared Owl, was flushed from the edge of the Upper Pond about Christmas, 1969. The Kingfisher, however, was very rarely noted.

The ordinary woodland birds, especially of the more common species, were seen everywhere. Six Stonechats were noted in October 1969, and 21 Whinchats during August and September. The Common Redstart continued to breed and Black Redstarts were seen in the spring of 1970. The observers believed that the fact that only one Singing Tree Pipit was heard or seen in each year was due to constant disturbance.

Warblers were in plenty, among them the Grasshopper Warbler, heard singing in the Lower Pen Pond plantation in April 1969, and the Reed Warblers, which maintain themselves in the reed beds at the head of the Upper Pond. Redpolls were numerous, but Siskins much less so. Other Finches and Buntings showed little change.

Among passerine (perching) birds, the event of the year, the report concludes, was the appearance of a Great Grey Shrike which stayed for a week in early November 1970. The foregoing gives a very fair cross-section of the widely differing bird life of Richmond Park which, only nine miles from the centre of London and now surrounded by buildings, manages to maintain a galaxy of different species of every size and many colours to delight the hearts of birdlovers.

One bird not to be found in Richmond Park today is the turkey, but, according to Edward Jesse, the naturalist who was Deputy Surveyor of the Royal Parks in the 1830s and '40s: 'In the reign of George III a large flock of wild turkeys was regularly kept up as part of the stock of Richmond Park and some of the turkey cocks are said to have weighed from 25 lb to 30 lb. They were hunted with dogs and made to take refuge in a tree where they were frequently shot at by the King. The whole stock was eventually destroyed about the end of the reign in consequence of many sanguinary contests having taken place between the keepers and the poachers, with respect to the chasing of these birds'.

The Animals

All the common woodland animals have been found in the park over the generations and many of them are still there today.

There are at least 2,000 grey squirrels and many rabbits, both regarded as vermin by those who look after the park, but very attractive to visitors. Hares and hedgehogs are comparatively rare, as are bats — though a few of the latter have been seen, mainly near Oak and Bog Lodges, in the dark of the evenings — and there are virtually no moles. Over the years, the mole, which must have been very prolific at the enclosure since, very early on, an official mole catcher was appointed, has grown rarer and rarer. Even in 1937, Collenette reported it was 'now an uncommon animal in the park'. And although pine martens and polecats were seen in the park up to the turn of the century, there is no record of them in recent times.

Stoats, weasels, shrews, field mice, voles, rats and foxes can all be found. There is believed to be a pair of badgers living in the Isabella Plantation at the present time and even the rare red squirrel is sometimes seen.

The Fish

On the park's several ponds, the fish life includes Tench, Carp, Roach, Pike and other 'coarse' species. The fish are not indigenous and during the past 20 years, the ponds have been regularly restocked from the Metropolitan Water Board Reservoirs.

The Bracken

A chapter on the natural history of the park must include a word or two about the bracken which, when it turns red-gold in the autumn, is a glorious sight. It has a practical use as well and if it was allowed to disappear, the bird and animal life of the park would be seriously affected.

An extract from an article by Collenette in *The London Naturalist* (journal of the London Natural History Society) in 1936, explains this very clearly:

'In the latter half of the last century, writers about the park frequently speak of the difficulty of forcing a way through the high bracken and one plant was mentioned as being 8 ft. 7 in. in height. ... At the present time, the most robust growth is little more than waist high and I have reason to think that it is still slowly deteriorating. The bracken was noticably poor in 1936 when the unusually late frost on 17th May withered the first shoots. ... Much of the bird life of the park is dependent on a sturdy and extensive growth of bracken. With the exception of the Juncus Communis and Juncus Glaucus, which flourished in the damp areas, bracken is the only plant affording ground cover which is not cropped by deer. Apart from the shelter afforded them at all seasons, these birds that nest on the ground are almost completely dependent on the withered bracken of the previous year for nesting cover and such species as Stonechat and Whinchat, Woodlark, Tree and Meadow Pipit, Yellow and Red Bunting, would completely disappear if deprived of the protection.'

Today, the bracken is certainly not 8 ft. 7 in. high, but profuse plantations of it can be found throughout the park, which should allay any fears that the deterioration noted by Collenette has seriously continued.

The Wild Flowers

Though the botanist appreciates the fact, most ordinary visitors to the park would be surprised to learn that there are — and always have been — literally hundreds of species of wild flowers growing abundantly. They range from the Wood Pansy to the Willow Herb and from the Thistle and Heath to the Water Plantain. An intriguing little book by H.R. Hall, published in 1923 'with the approval and sanction of His Majesty's Office of Works,' records most of them. Mr. Hall began his series of observations in 1890 and he points out in the preface to the book that the park in 1922 was in some respects very different from what it was in 1890. He may possibly have meant this statement only to apply to the species and abundancy of the wild flowers he observed but it could, in fact, mean all the wild life, both flora and fauna.

The Old Shrew Ash in the 18th century ... and in the 20th.

VII

RICHMOND PARK TODAY

KING CHARLES I allowed poor people to enter his park to gather firewood. Possibly he had a guilty conscience about taking their common land and perhaps he wanted to recapture some of his lost popularity. Today, 334 years later, the Department of the Environment carries on this tradition. Local people may still claim the privilege of gathering firewood and apply to the Superintendent for a 'wood permit'.

Few other traditions remain and the story is essentially one of change. There are still six carriage gates and five pedestrian gates, but some of the houses have gone and others are used for different purposes. Except for Princess Alexandra and her family at Thatched House Lodge, no 'private' individual lives in the park. The historic White Lodge has been occupied since 1954 by the boarding school of the Royal Ballet School. The Superintendent and his family live in a flat in Pembroke Lodge, the ground floor of which has been turned into a public restaurant and snack bar, and it is surrounded by gardens in which the public can wander. Bog Lodge (once Holly Lodge and a farm, which it still resembles) is the office of the Superintendent and his staff and the horses ridden by the two mounted girl park-keepers are stabled there.

The lodges at the carriage gates are occupied by the keeper and his wife — who is often also a keeper — and there are keepers and their families in the other dwelling-houses set about the park. A large staff of keepers, foresters and workmen run and look after the park. Keepers in Landrovers patrol it regularly and the two mounted keepers traverse it several times a day.

Sport has today become an important feature of Richmond Park.

Horse riding is allowed up to 1 p.m. on Monday to Friday

16. Red deer in the bracken

17. A mounted girl park keeper pauses by one of the Pen Ponds

18. Aquatic scene in the Isabella Woodland Garden

19. Some of the sheep that graze in the park

20. One of the oak trees that stood before the 1637 enclosure

or until 11 a.m. on Saturdays, Sundays and bank holidays anywhere except the enclosed areas, foot paths and areas of mown grass. At other times, horse riding must be confined to the road or the riding tracks around the park and the riding ring.

There is a polo ground and both kinds of football can be played on several pitches, all of which can be hired and are in constant use. Model boats can be sailed on Adam's Pond, near Sheen Gate, and Ham Dip Pond, near Ham Gate. There is even a small area set aside for flying powered model aircraft. Skating is permitted on all the ponds but only when the ice is at least five inches thick on Pen Ponds and three inches thick on the other smaller and shallower ponds.

Two 18-hole golf courses, Duke's Course and Prince's Course, with another public restaurant attached, have been laid out between Roehampton and Robin Hood Gate. Some of the older golfers remember that on 30 August 1931, the London General Omnibus Company started a special bus route, No. 207, to bring golfers from Barnes Station into the park and deposit them at the golf courses. The one-man-operated bus ran from the Railway Hotel by the station via Roehampton Lane and Clarence Lane. On the return journey, it came down Priory Lane. With a 15-minute service on weekdays and a 10-minute service on Saturdays and Sundays, the journey took six minutes and cost 3d. each way. The service ran uninterrupted, one of the very few ever to go right inside a Royal Park, until 17 October 1939, when it became a casualty of the Second World War. It has never been resumed and most golfers today arrive in their own cars.

There are nine big car parks in the park today; one of them, at Broomfield Hill, includes a restaurant kiosk. Parking elsewhere is forbidden.

The public may picnic in the park, play ball games and fly kites, but they must not play radios or record players, pick flowers or foliage, leave litter about, frighten or chase the deer or allow their dogs to do so. They must not feed the deer and must not disturb them, particularly in the rutting (mating) season in October and November, when they may be fierce if approached. There are, in essence, surprisingly few prohibitions on the public's use of the park and those rules that are in force are, on the whole very well respected.

The park is open throughout the hours of daylight every day of the year and, after dark, pedestrians can be admitted if they wish to use the park as a thoroughfare, which is very unlikely in these days. It remains a constant delight in every season for local people and visitors alike and a tribute to those who, over the years, have worked to preserve and enhance its beauty.

APPENDIX

THE RANGERS AND SUPERINTENDENTS

AT LEAST three of the books written exclusively about the park which I have consulted (*A History of Richmond New Park by a Resident* — 1877; *The Handbook of Richmond Park* by Coryn de Vere — 1909; and *A History of Richmond Park* by C.L. Collenette* — 1937) and most of the Surrey histories have some inaccuracies in the list of Rangers of the park appointed by the reigning monarch from 1637 until the death of King Edward VII in 1910.

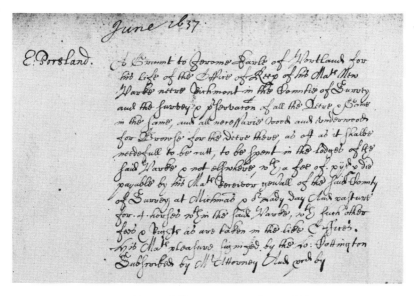

From Signet Office Docquets, June 1637
reproduced by courtesy of Public Record Office

67

Most of the evidence is in original documents kept at the Public Record Office. Here is what I believe to be the first accurate and complete list of Rangers that has been compiled.

Jerome, Earl of Portland	1637–1649[1]
No Ranger during the Commonwealth	1649–1660
Sir Lionel Tollemache and his wife,	
Elizabeth, Countess of Dysart	1660–1668[2]
Sir Daniel Harvey (in absence)	1668–1672[3]
John, Duke of Lauderdale	1673–1683[4]
Laurence Hyde, Earl of Rochester	1683–1711[5]
Henry Hyde, Earl of Rochester	
(held in his name by Francis	
Gwyn Esqre and Richard Powys,	
gent)	1711–1727[6]
Robert, Lord Walpole	1727–1751[7]
Princess Amelia	1751–1761[8]
John, Earl of Bute	1761–1792[9]
King George III	1792–1814[10]
Princess Elizabeth	1814–1835[11]
Adolphus Frederick, Duke	
of Cambridge	1835–1850[12]
Princess Mary, Duchess of	
Gloucester	1850–1857[13]
George, Duke of Cambridge	1857–1904[14]
King Edward VII (through the	
first Commissioner of Works)	1904–1910[15]
Rangership lapses and	
Commissioners of Works take	
over	1910

Among the keepers appointed during and since George I's reign, the two families of Lucas and Sawyer were nearly always represented. A 'Mr. Lucas' was head keeper in George I's reign, though his dates are not known. His son, John Lucas, became head keeper after his death and, probably while George III was Ranger, was re-named Park Superintendent to run the working side of the park. Ever since then, there has always been a salaried Superintendent of the park, appointed after 1872 by the Commissioners of Works. There have been 10 Superintendents to date. All are listed in the records of the Department of the Environment and, except for the first date (1792), engraved on a board in the Superintendent's office in Bog Lodge in Richmond Park.

John Lucas	1792 (?)—1795
James Sawyer	1795—1825
James Sawyer	
(son of above)	1825—1872
Henry G. Sawyer	1872—1904
S. Pullman	1904—1919
B. Wells	1919—1927
R.W. Lucas	1928—1931
A.E. Wilson	1931—1951
George J. Thomson, M.V.O.	1951—1971
Michael Baxter Brown	1971—

SOURCES OF INFORMATION ABOUT THE RANGERS

1. Signet Office Docquets. Charles I. June 1637.
2. Cal. S.P. Dom. Charles II. 1660—61. p. 142.
3. Ibid. p. 210, and Signet Office Docquets. Charles II. August, 1660. Vol. XI p. 35.
4. Signet Office Docquets. Charles II. May, 1673. Vol. XVI
5. Ibid. October, 1683. Vol XVIII.
6. Ibid. Queen Anne. September, 1711.
7. Ibid. George II. October, 1727.
8. Patent Rolls. George II. 15—34. February 14, 1749.
9. Signet Office Docquets. George III. June, 1761.
10. Manning and Bray.
11. Signet Office Docquets. George III. May, 1814. and Patent Rolls. George III. 44—45. 1814.
12. Patent Rolls. William IV. September 10, 1835.
13. Ibid. Victoria. Part 1, No. 16. November 12, 1850.

14. Ibid. No. 4998. July 13, 1857.
15. Letter from Schomberg K. McDonnell, 1st Commissioner of Works, March 24, 1904, to Lord Knollys, and a note from King Edward VII, May 1, 1904. (both on Ministry of Works file 'Royal Parks.' P.R.O. REF: 16/215)

INDEX

Adam, Baron William of Blair Adam
42
Adam's Pond, Sheen Gate 42, 65
Albert, Prince Consort 36, 42
Aldridge, Charles 42
Aldridge's Lodge 42, 48
Alexandra, Princess 42, 64
Amelia (Amelie), Princess 28, 29, 30,
31, 46, 49, 51
Animals (small) 61, 62
Anne, Queen 25, 26
Argyle, Duchess of 48, 49
Army 16, 17, 39, 40, 51
Ash, Old Shrew 56
Auxiliary Territorial Service (A.T.S.)
40

Barnes 52, 65
Bateson, Lt. Gen. R., CVO 37
Bell, Mrs. G.A. 34
Bessborough, Earl of 49
Beverley Brook 45, 46, 47
Beverley Plaine 44, 45
Birds (species) 58, 59, 60, 61
Blacke Heathe 44, 45, 49
Bog Gate (also called Queen's Private
Gate) 47, 49, 50, 52
Bog Lodge (previously Holly Lodge)
51, 61, 64
Boleyn, Queen Anne 47, 48
Bowater, Gen. Sir Edward and Lady
42
Box Tree Wood 51
Bracken 62, 63
Breda, Holland 18
Brentford Ferry 2
Brooke, Lord 29
Broomfield Hill 51, 65

Brown, Lancelot (Capability) 32
Burkitt (or Burchett), John 42
Burkitt's (or Burchett's, Burcher's,
Burches) Lodge 42
Burgess, Deborah 29
Burrett, T. 49
Bute, John, Earl of 31, 32

Cambridge, Adolphus Frederick,
1st Duke of 35, 36
Cambridge, George, 2nd Duke of
37
Canterbury, Archbishop of (1894)
37
Carlile, Lodowick 10, 12, 15, 16,
17, 21
Carew, Sir George and Lady 47
Caroline, Queen (Consort of
George II) 27, 28, 29
Charles I 1, 2, 4, 5, 6, 7, 8, 9, 10,
11, 12, 13, 14, 19, 24, 30, 44,
45, 48, 64
Charles II 13, 15, 18, 19, 20, 21,
22, 23
Charlotte, Queen (Consort of
George III) 32
Chohole Gate 47, 49, 50
Chohole Field 50
Clarence Lane, Roehampton 65
Clarendon, Edward Hyde, 1st Earl
of 4, 5, 6, 7, 8
Clarendon, Henry (Harry) Hyde,
2nd Earl of 24, 25, 26, 27
Clifton, General 36
Cole, Gregory 12
Collenette, C.L. 58, 59, 61, 62
Conduit Game Preserve 51
Constitution Hill 21

71